I am grateful to God for everything! And I believe that the meaning of life is to make sense of other lives. C.A., you are the meaning of my life.
Lov U

Madison Swift
2024

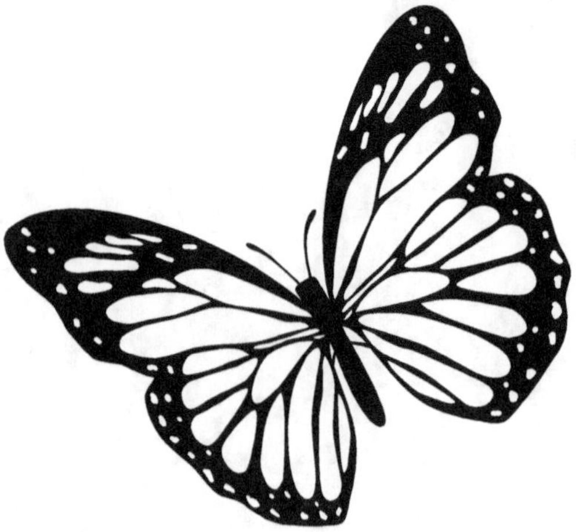
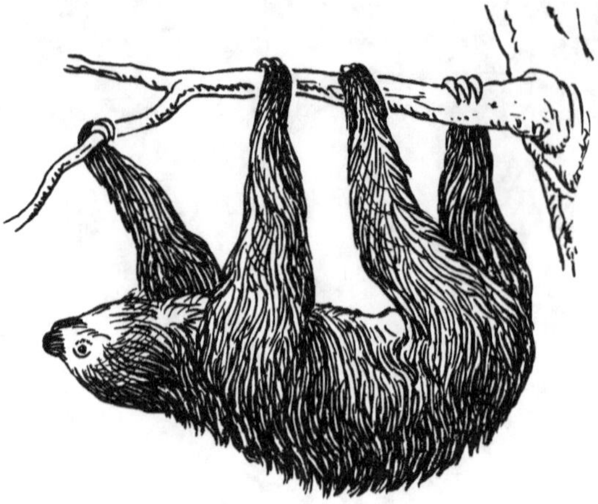

This Book Belongs to:

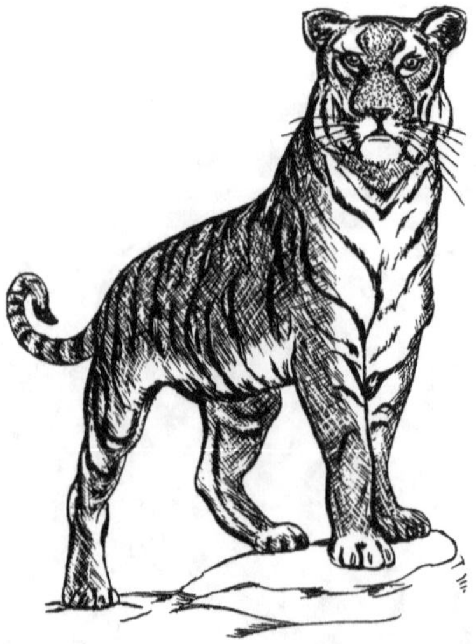
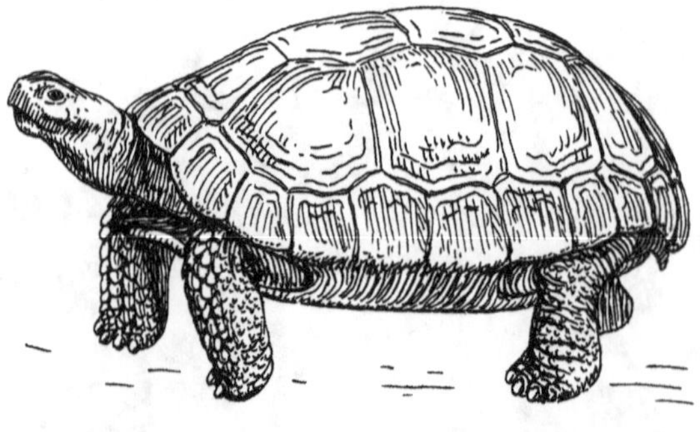

M.P.D.©
Madison's Poets Department

Test Color Page

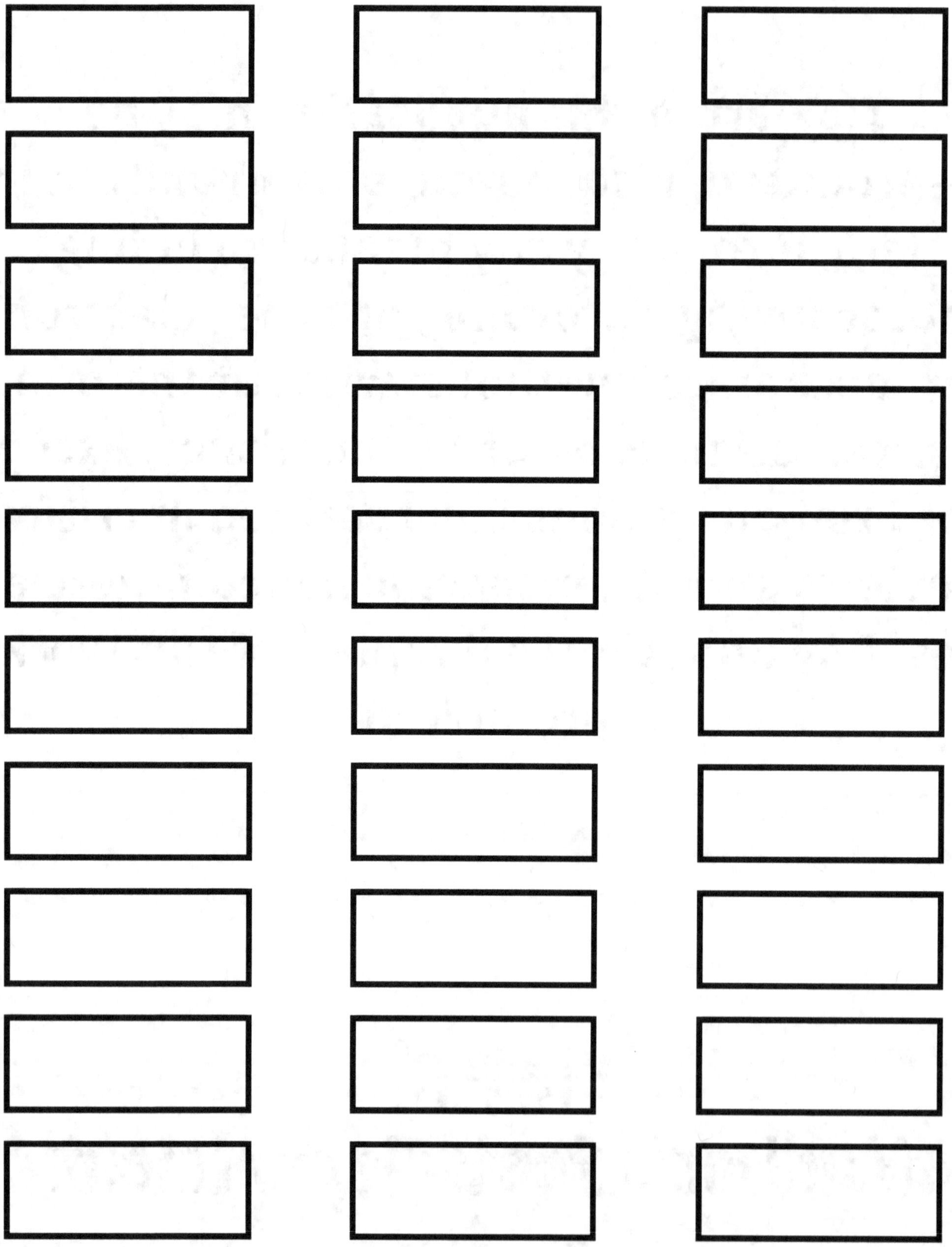

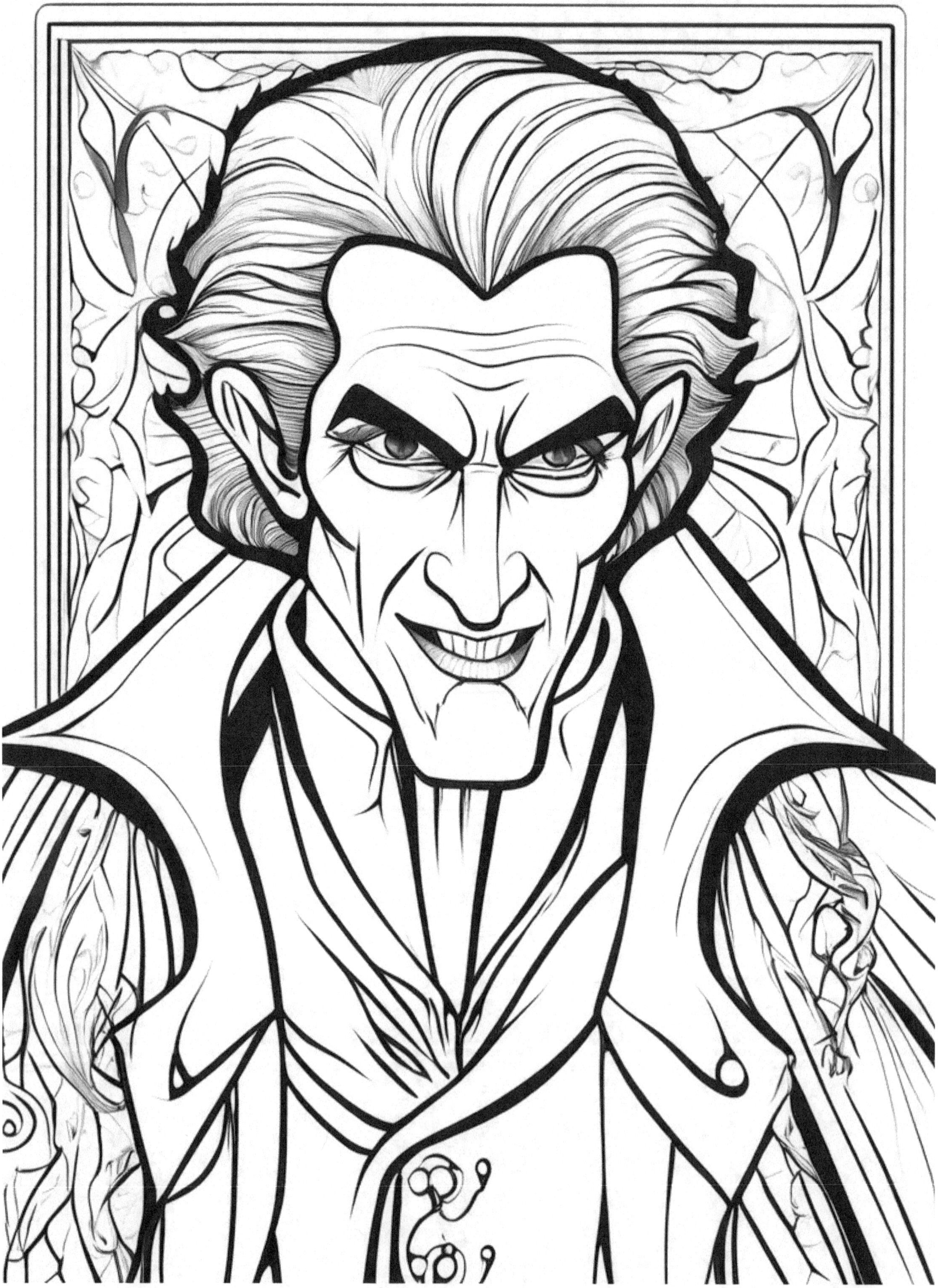

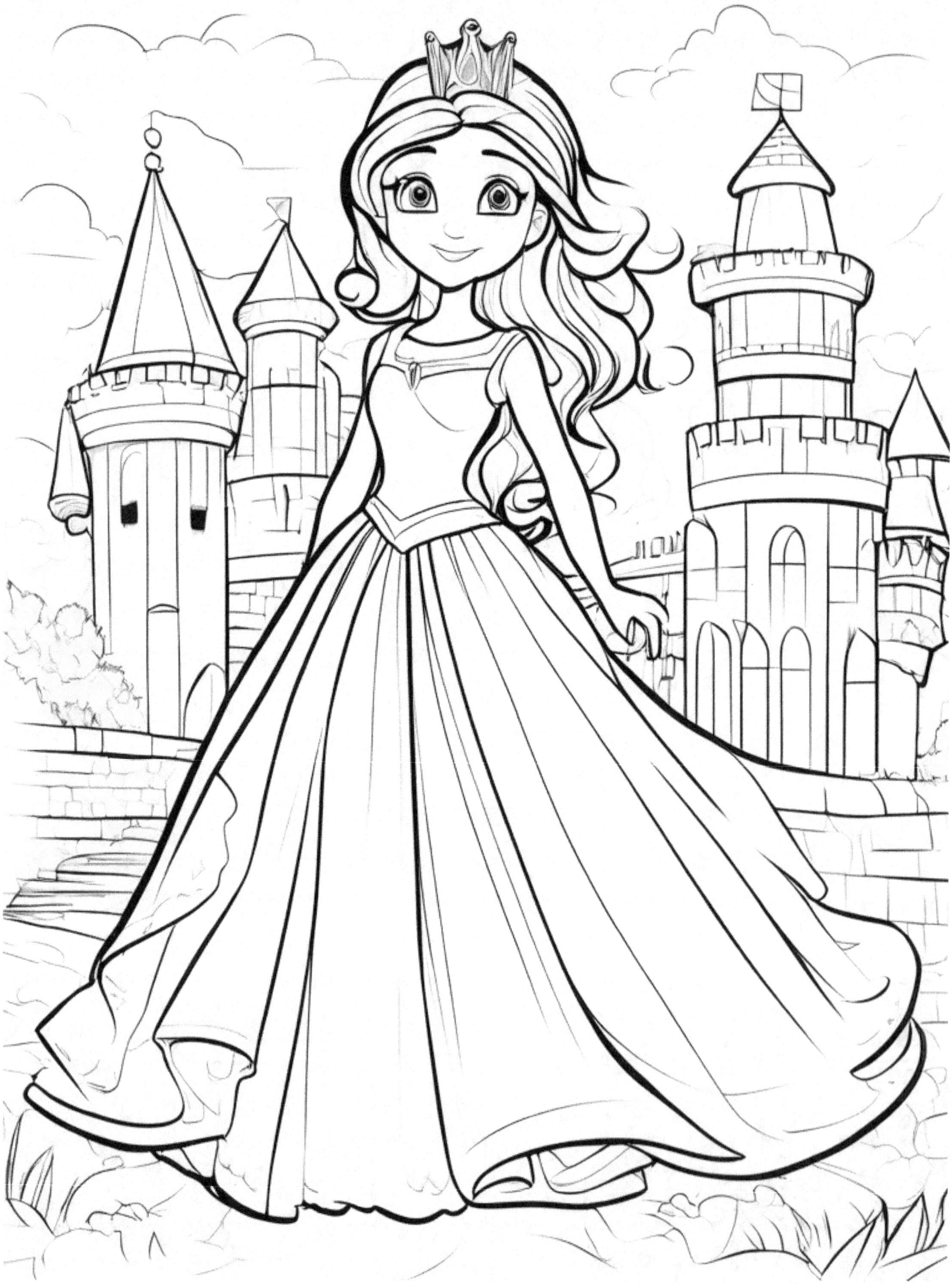

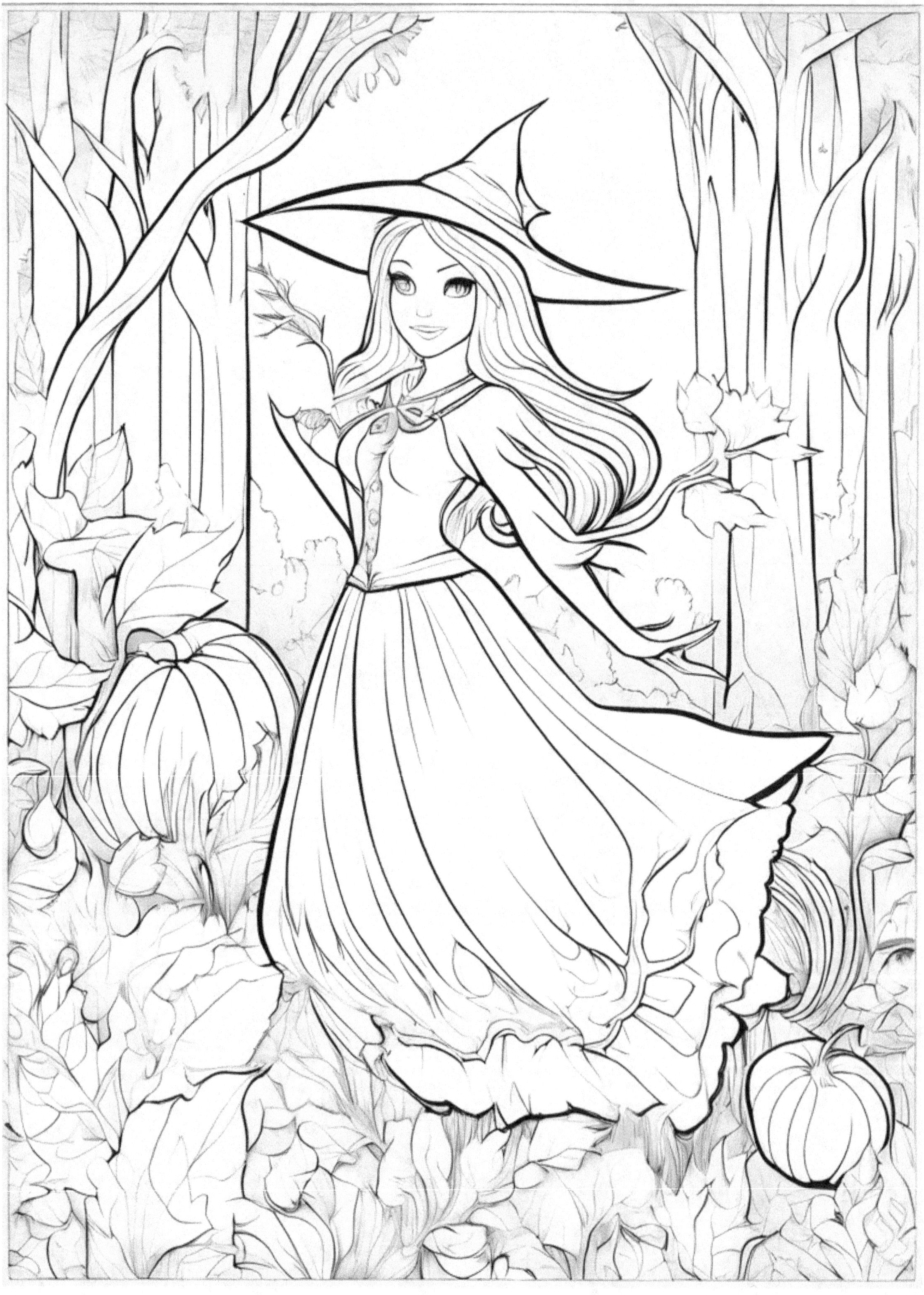

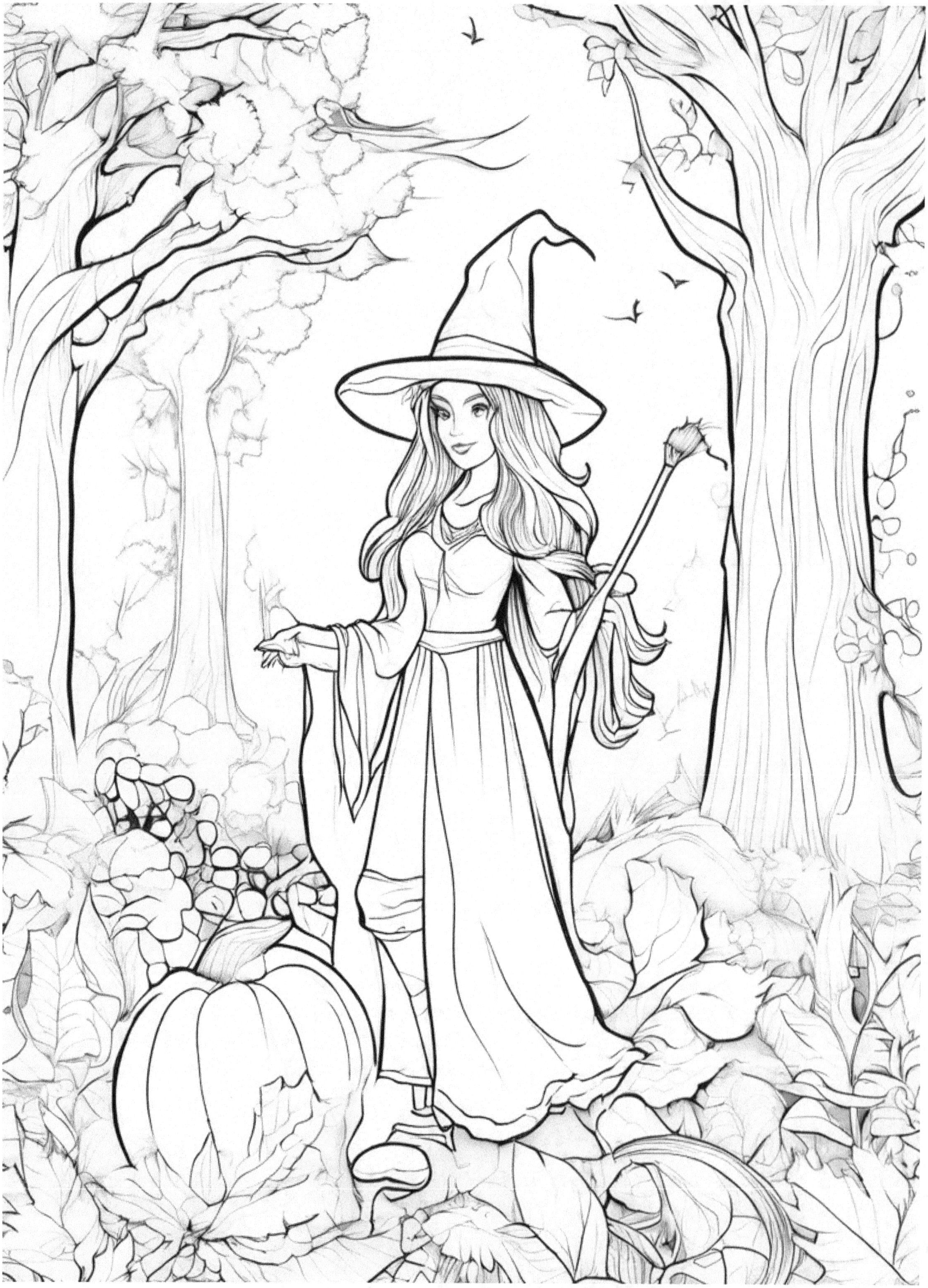

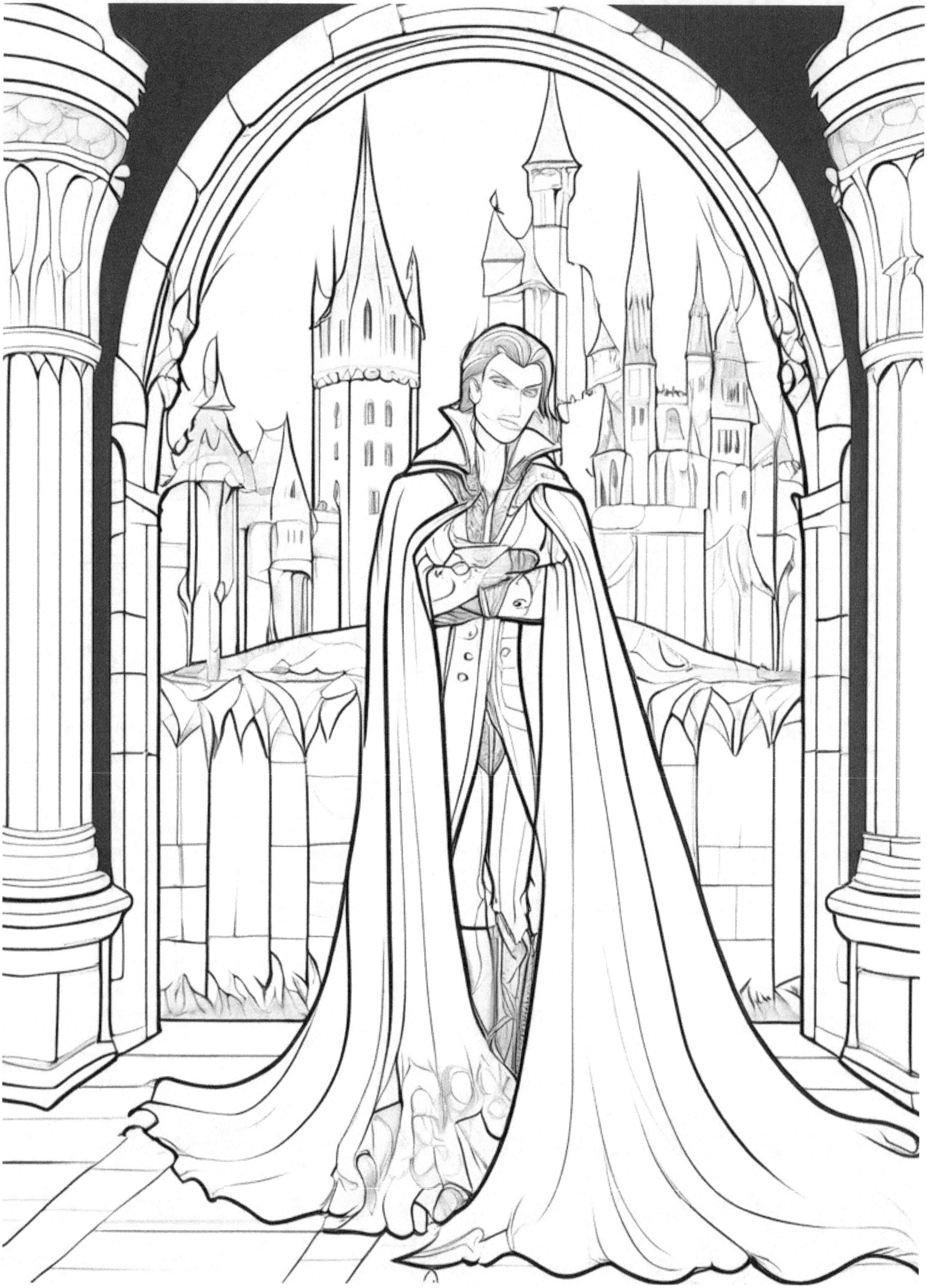

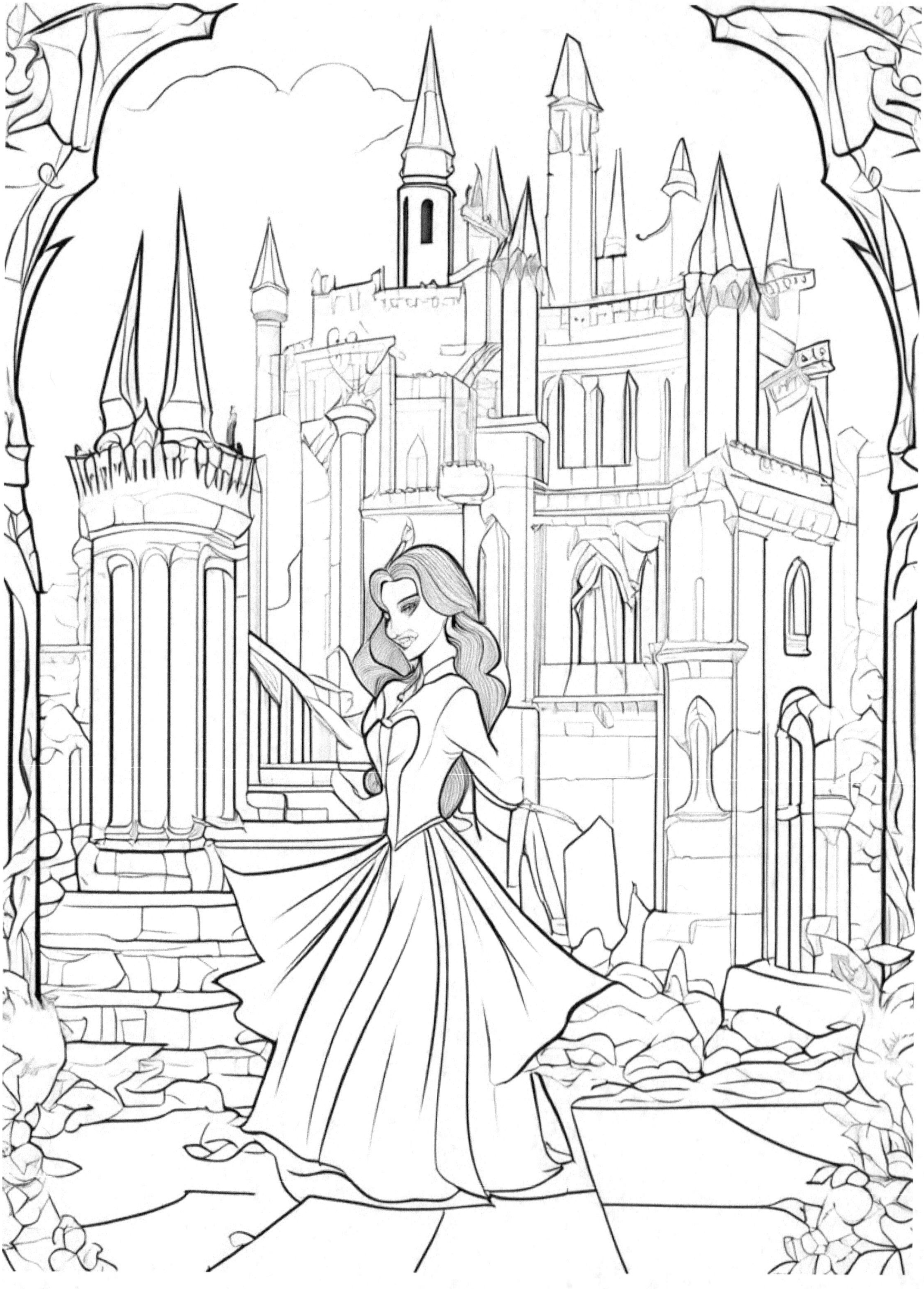

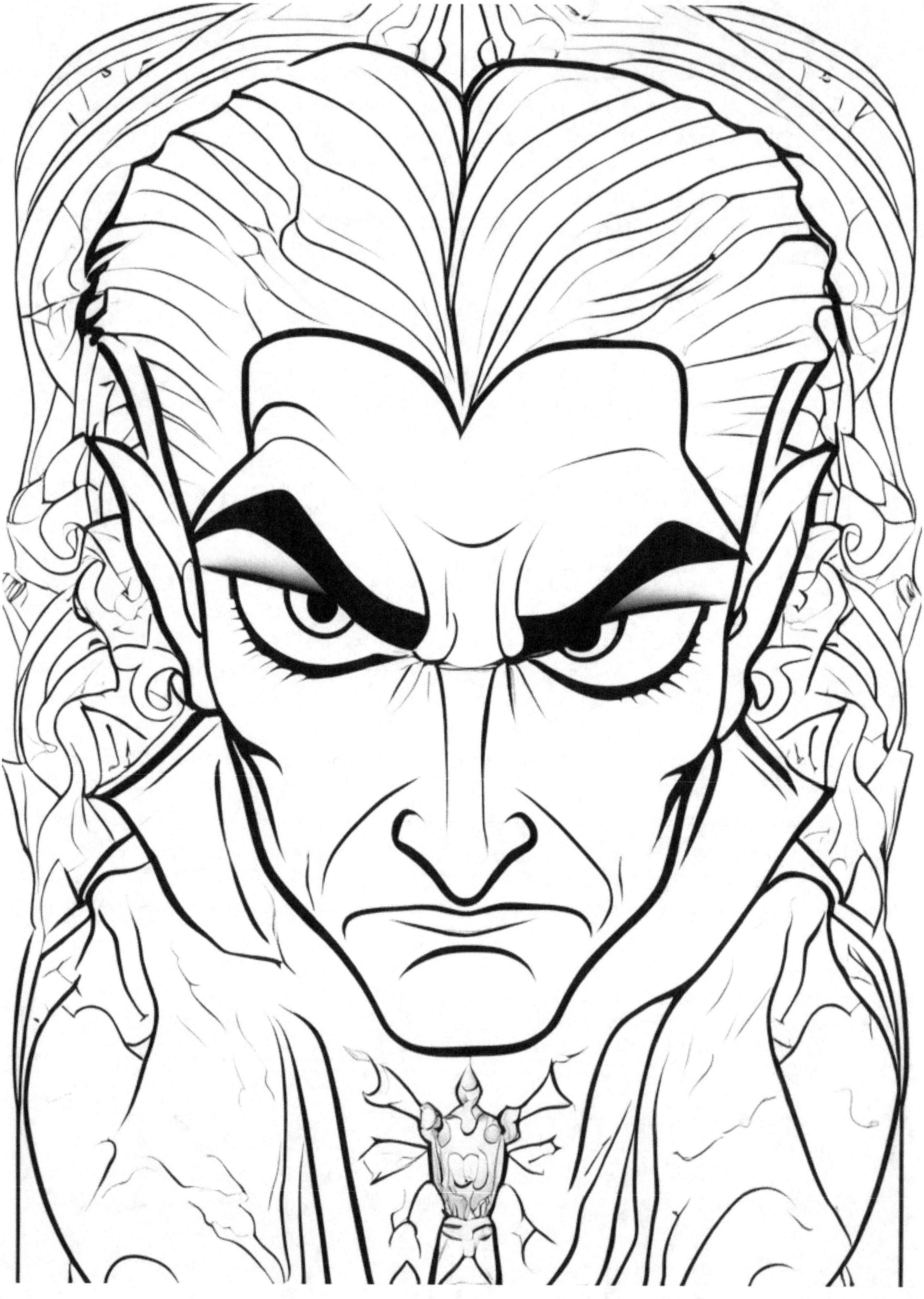

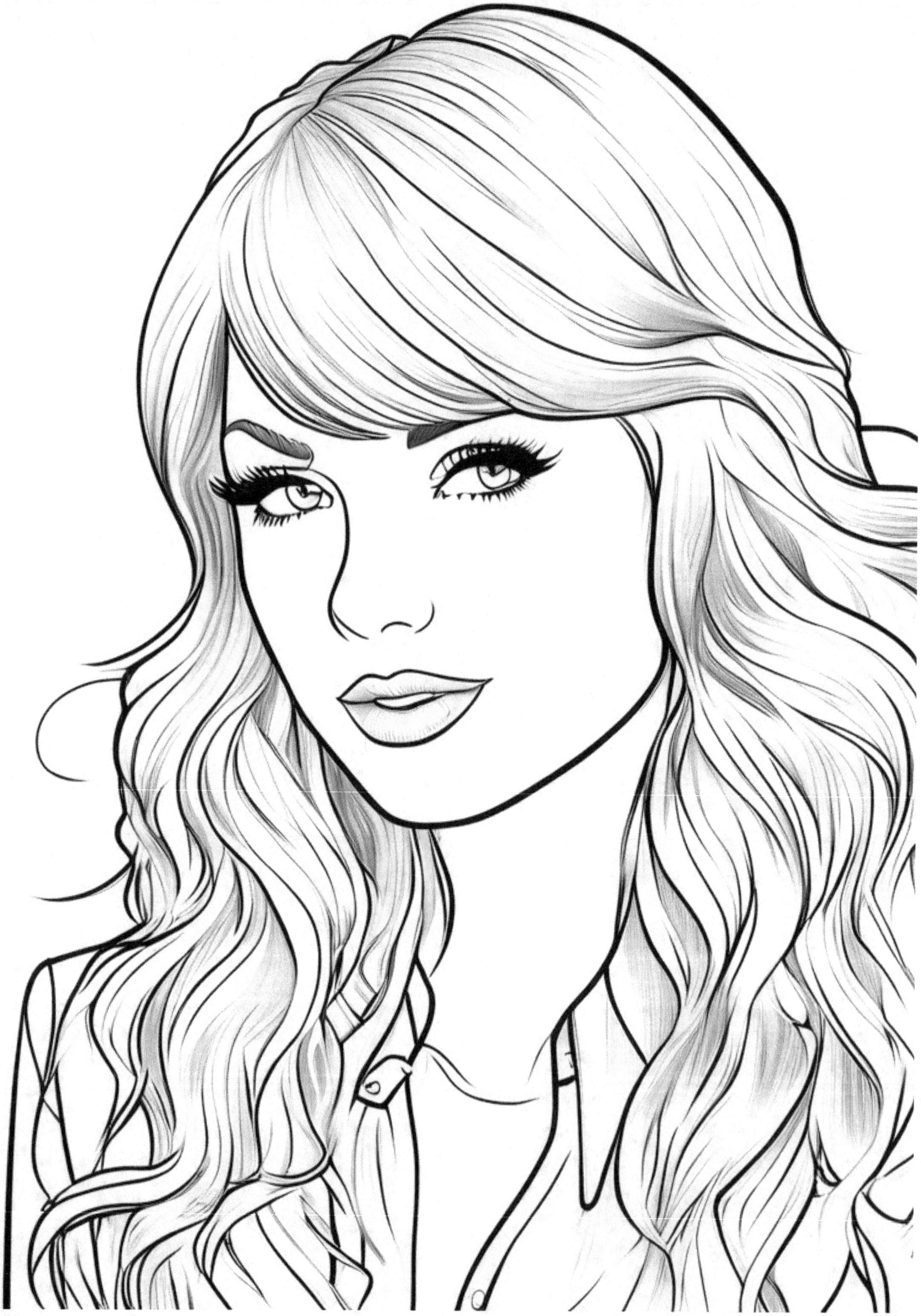

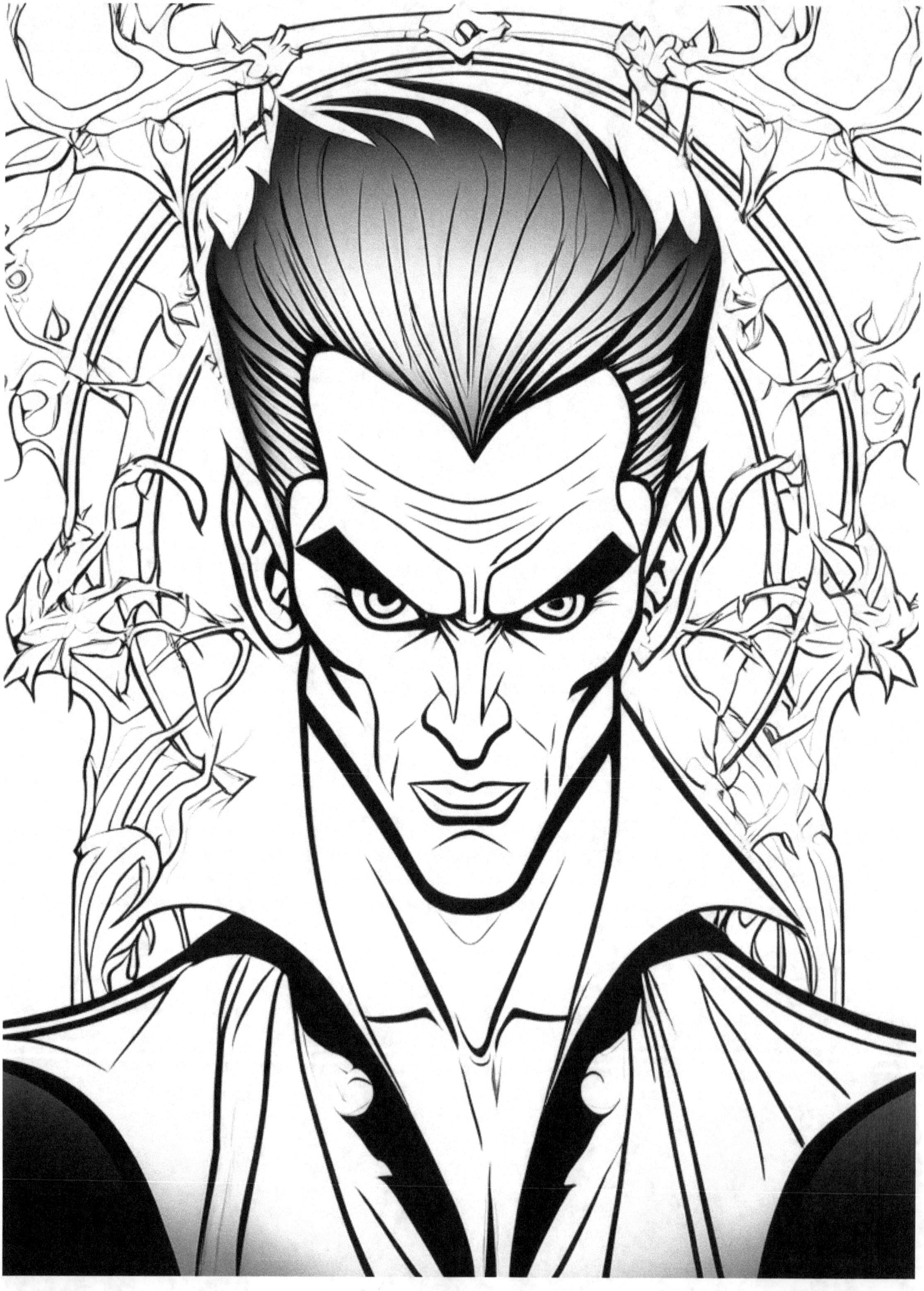

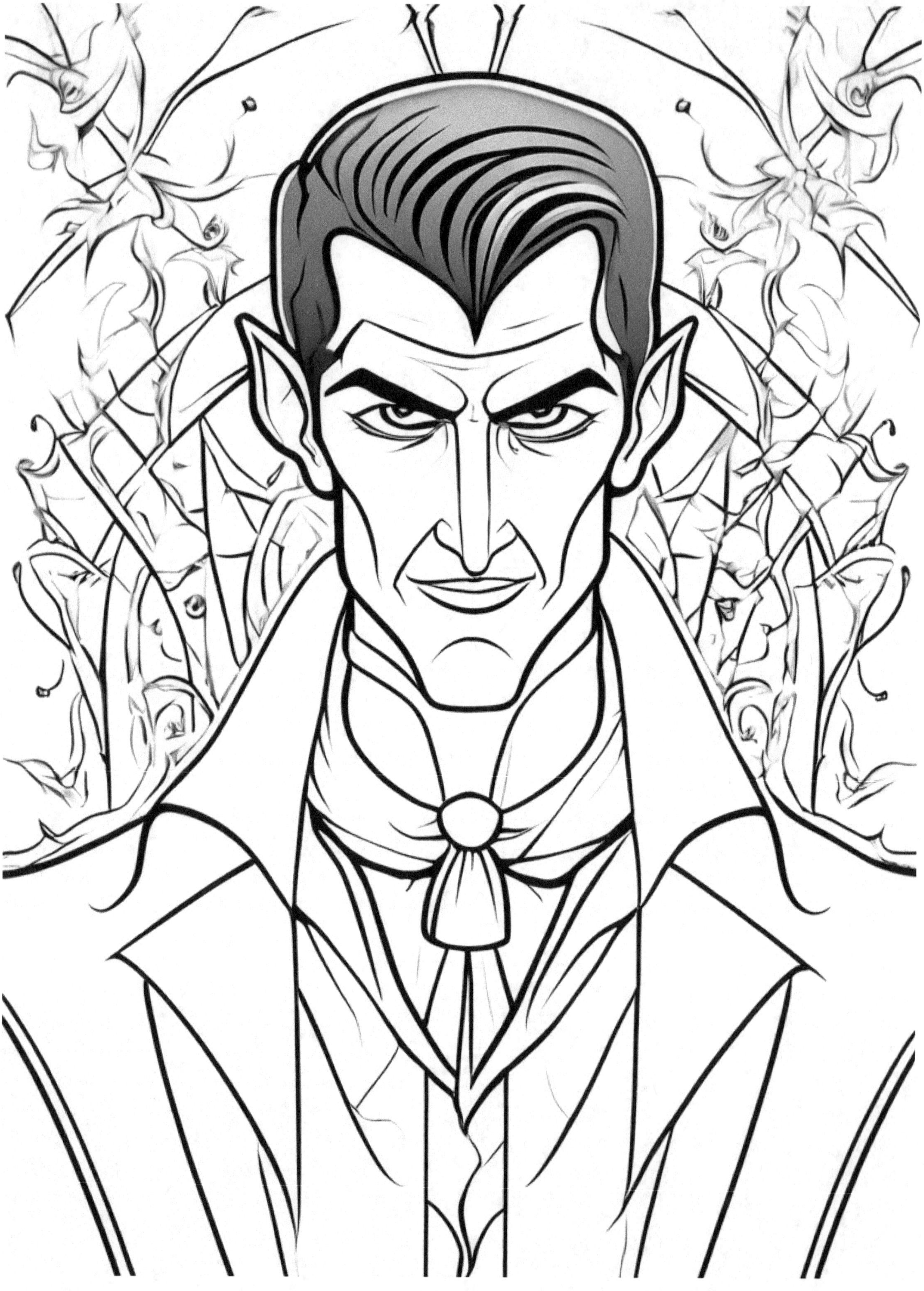

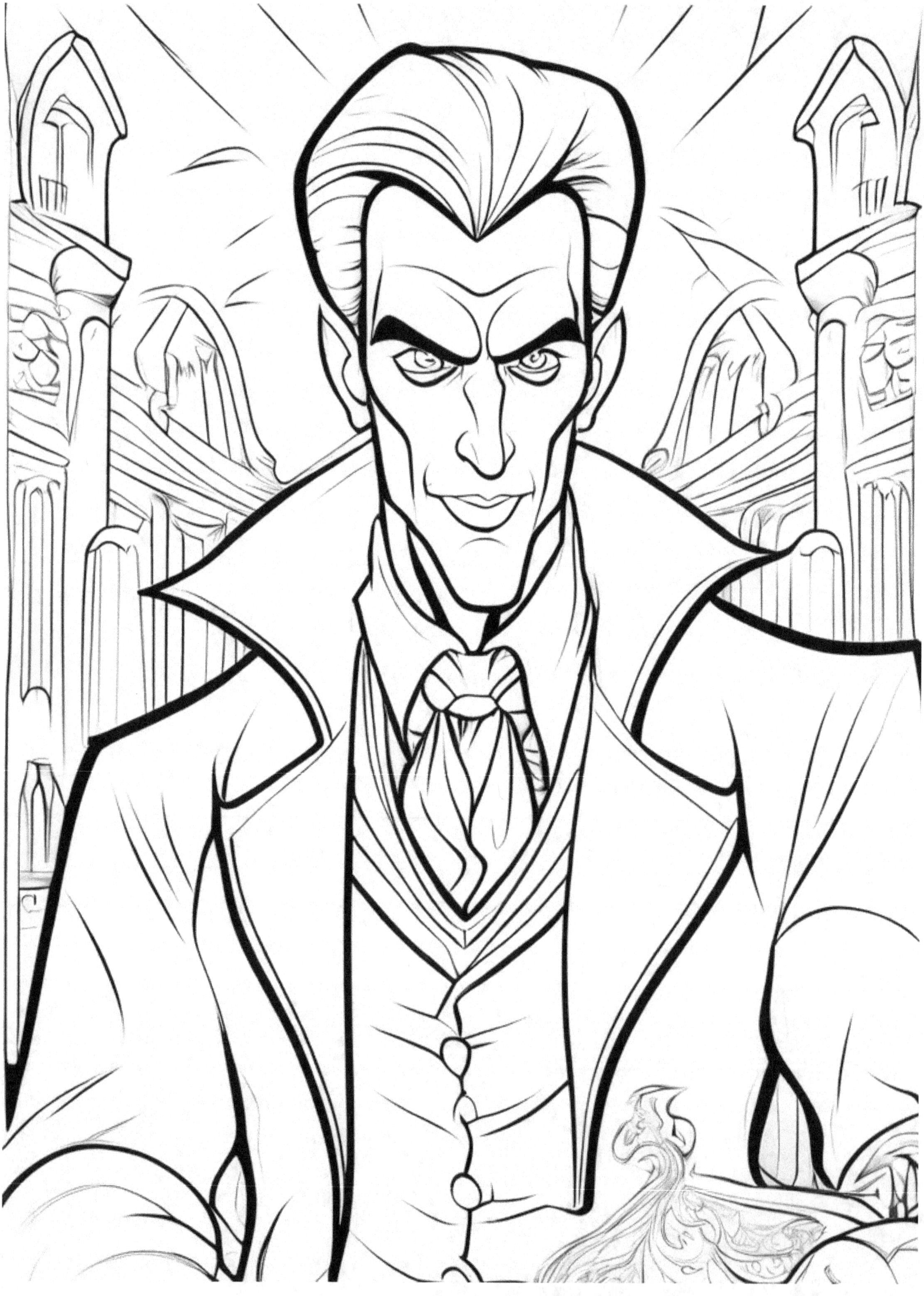

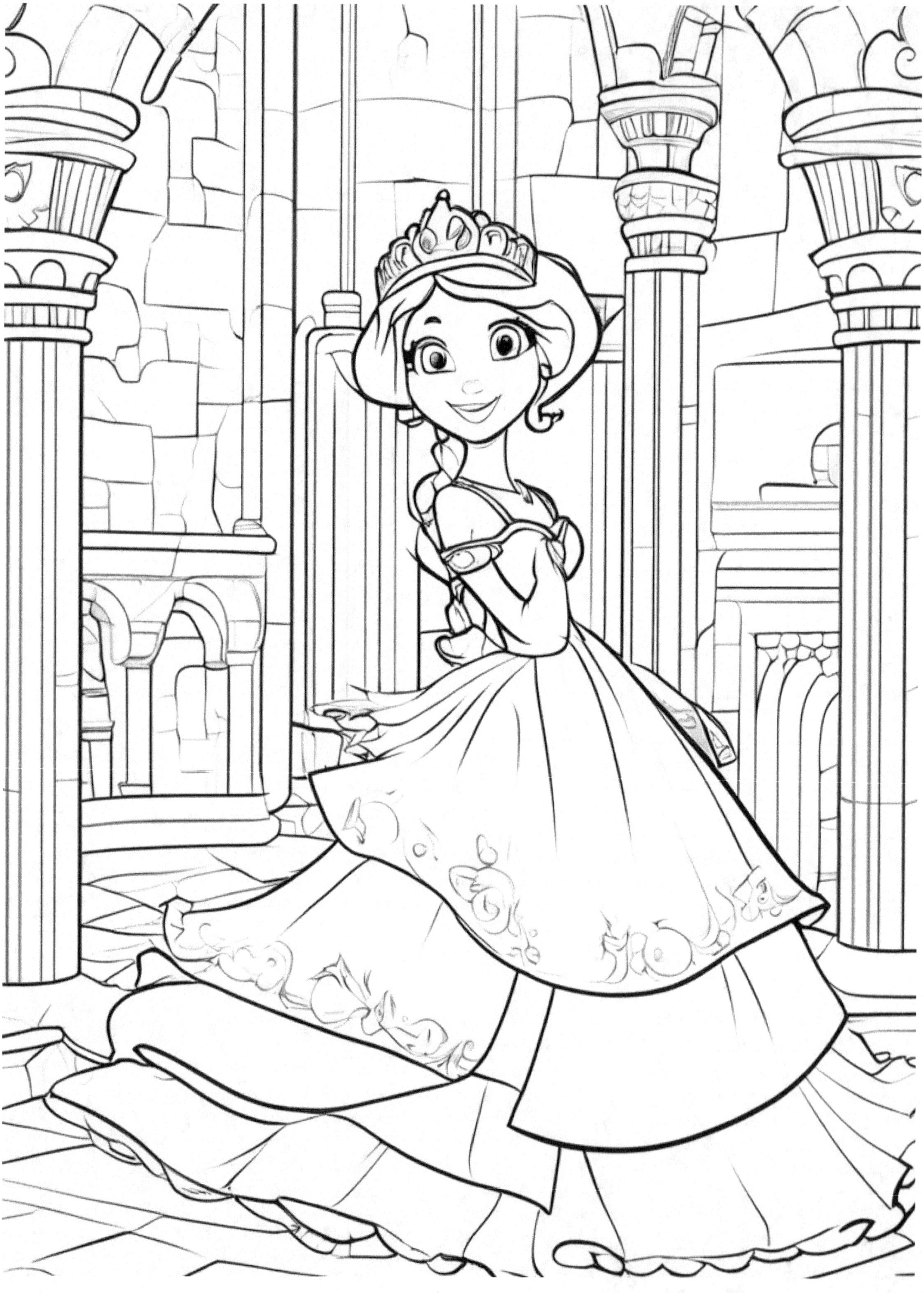

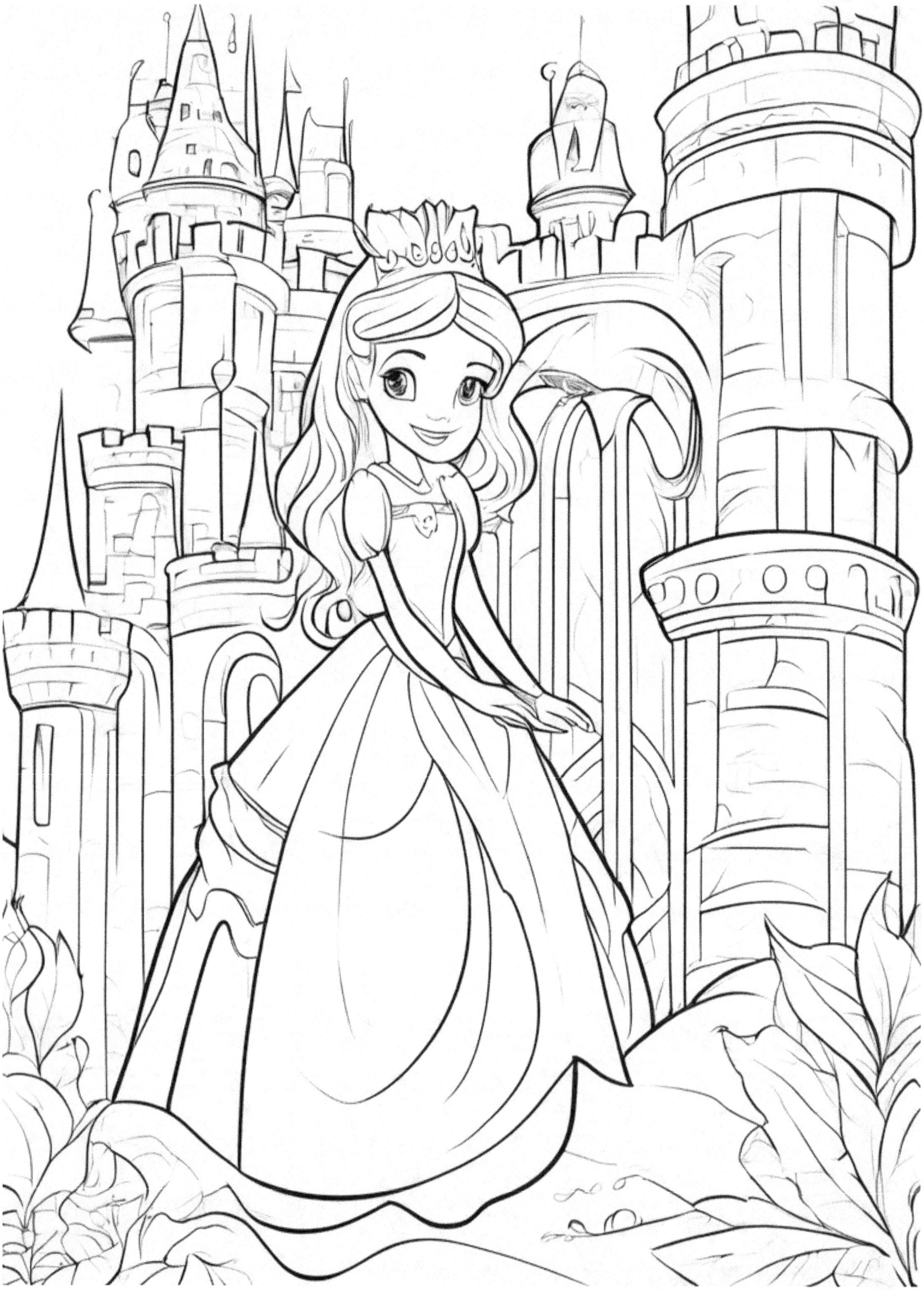

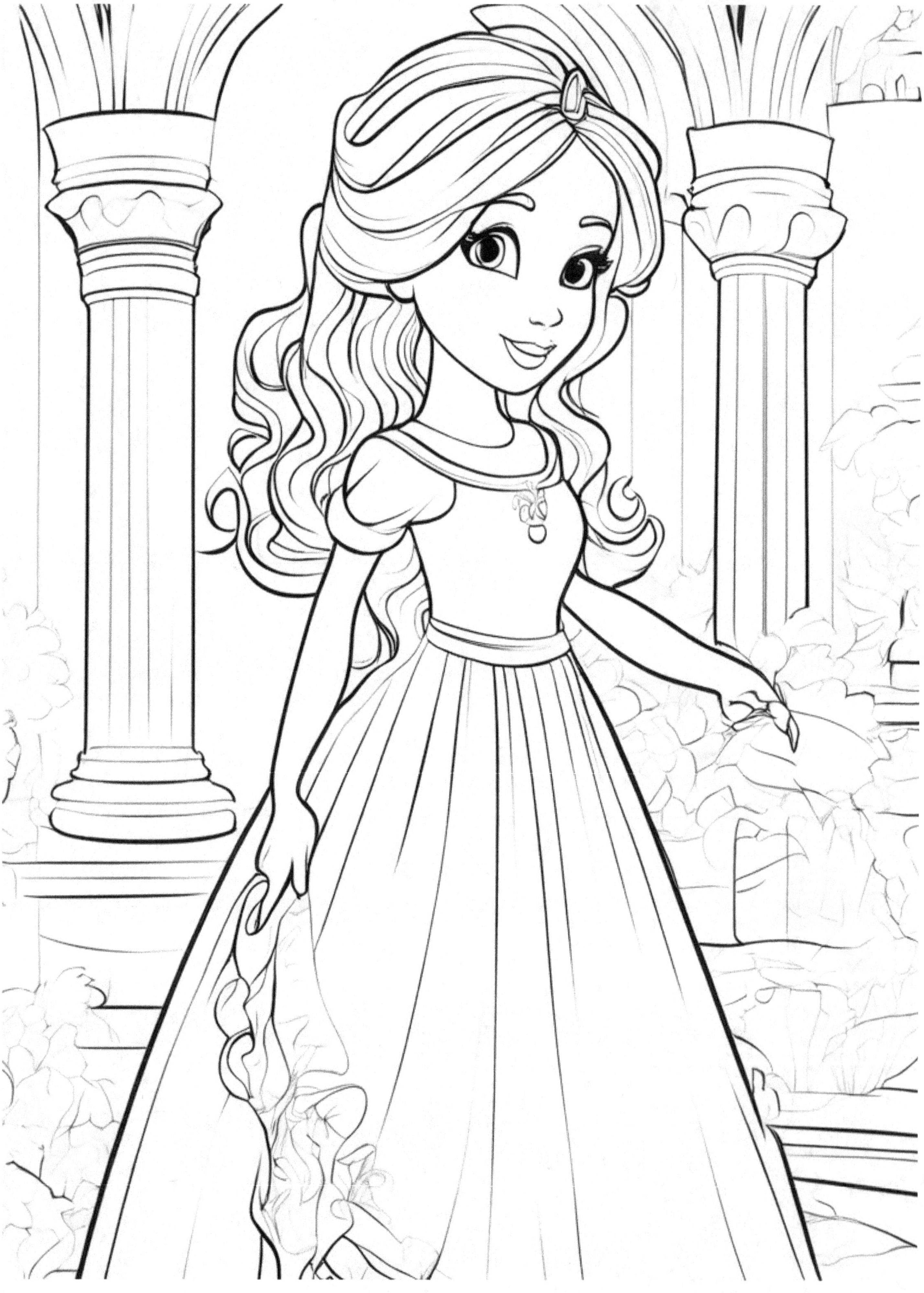

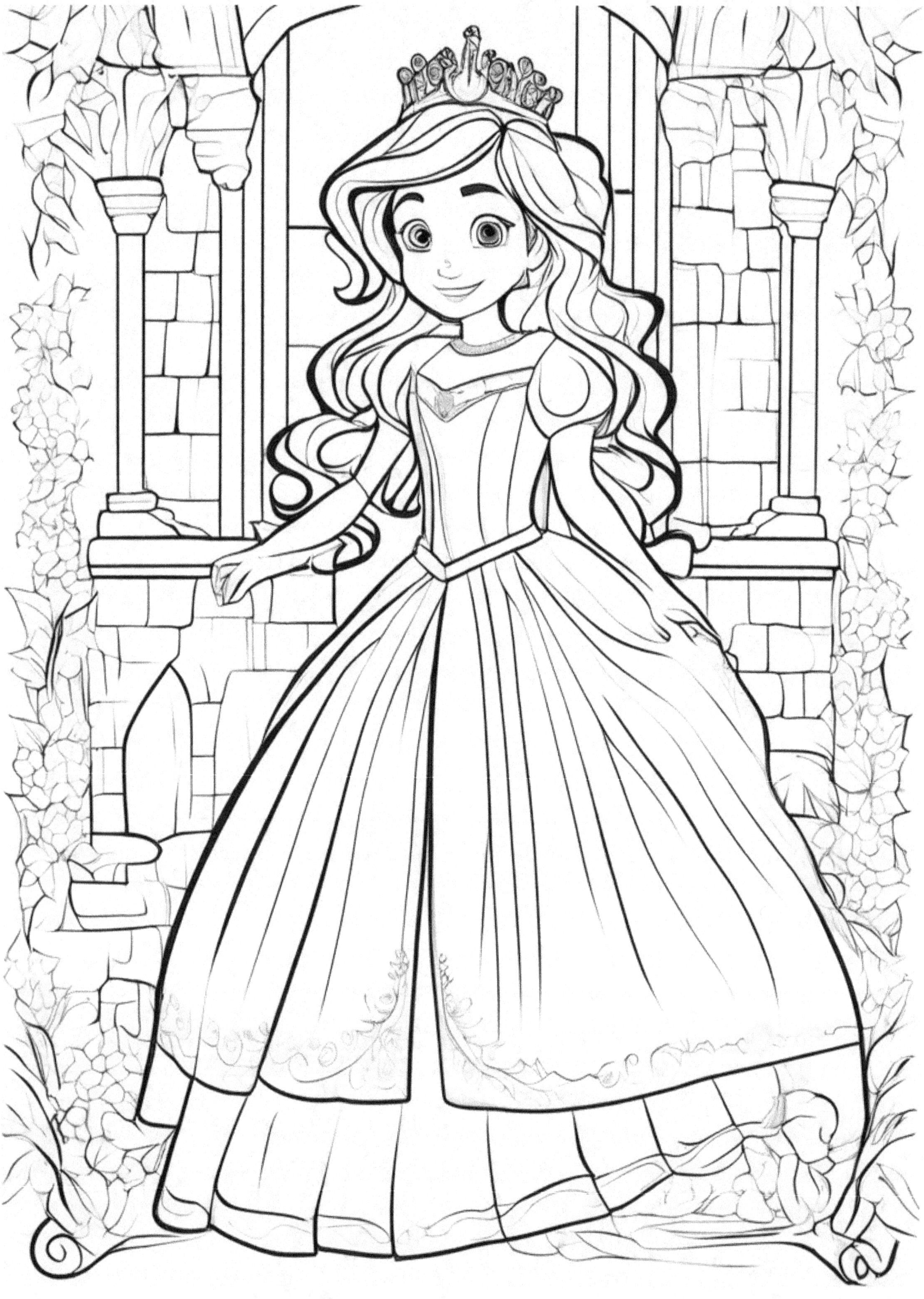

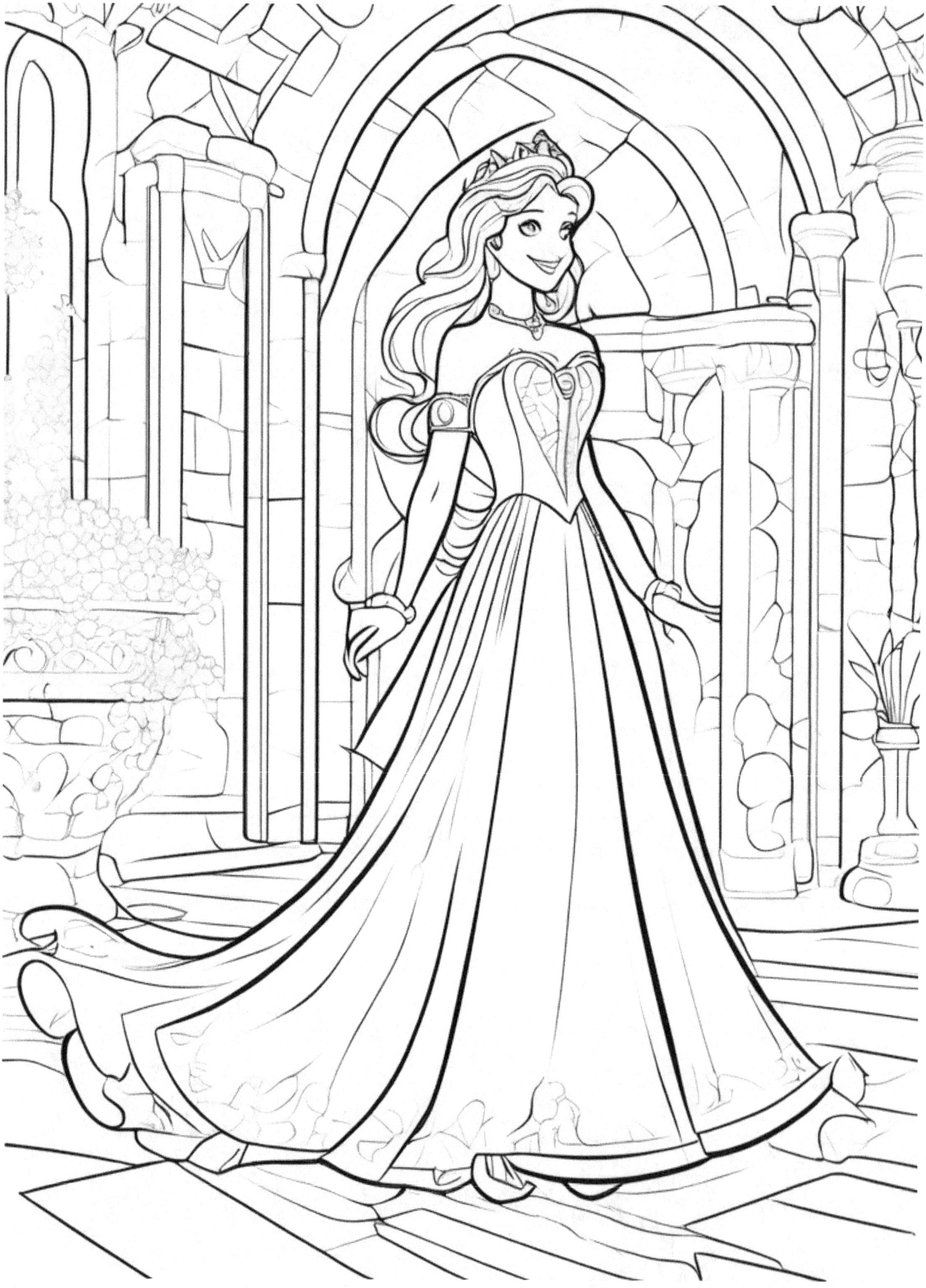

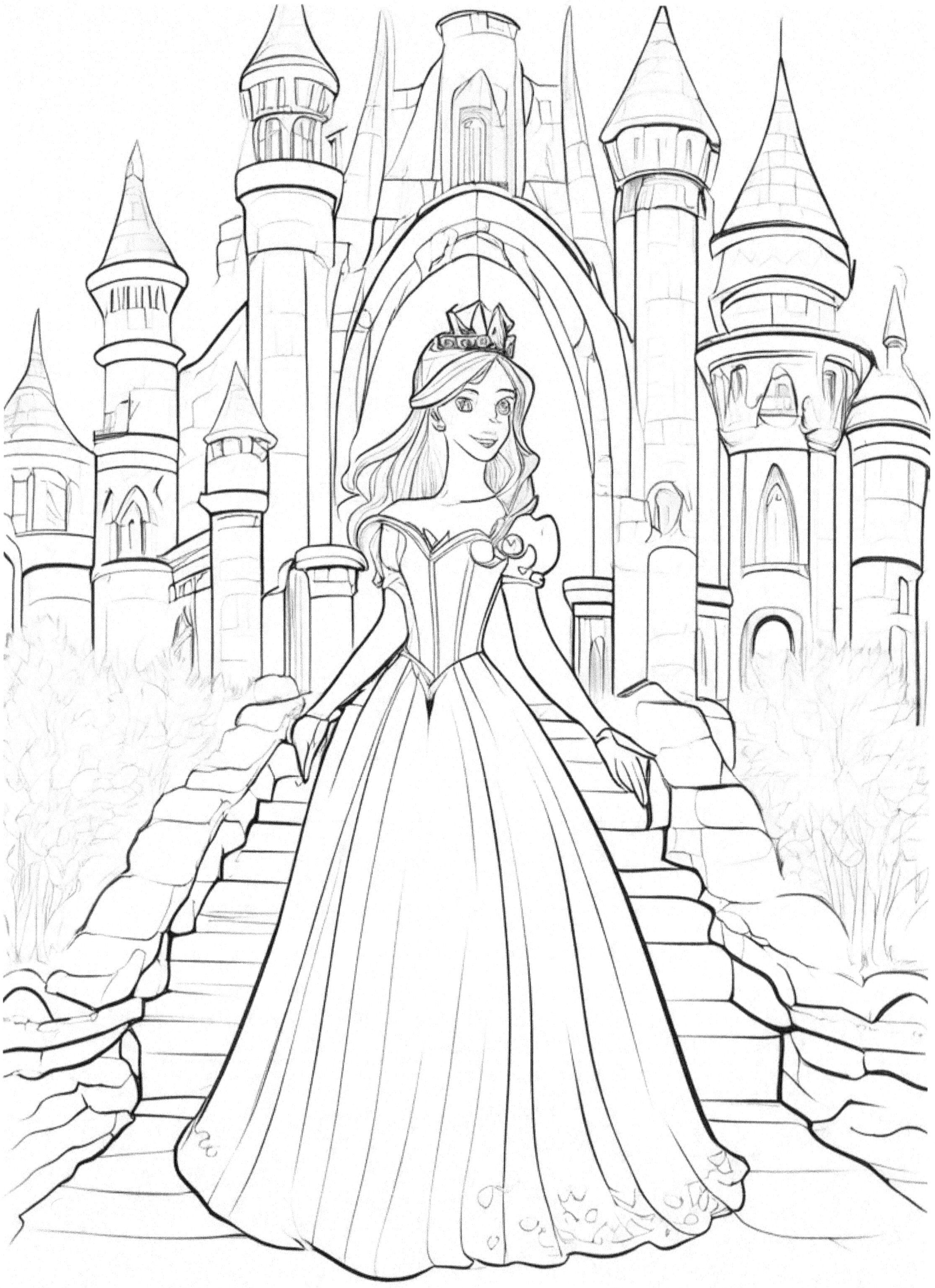

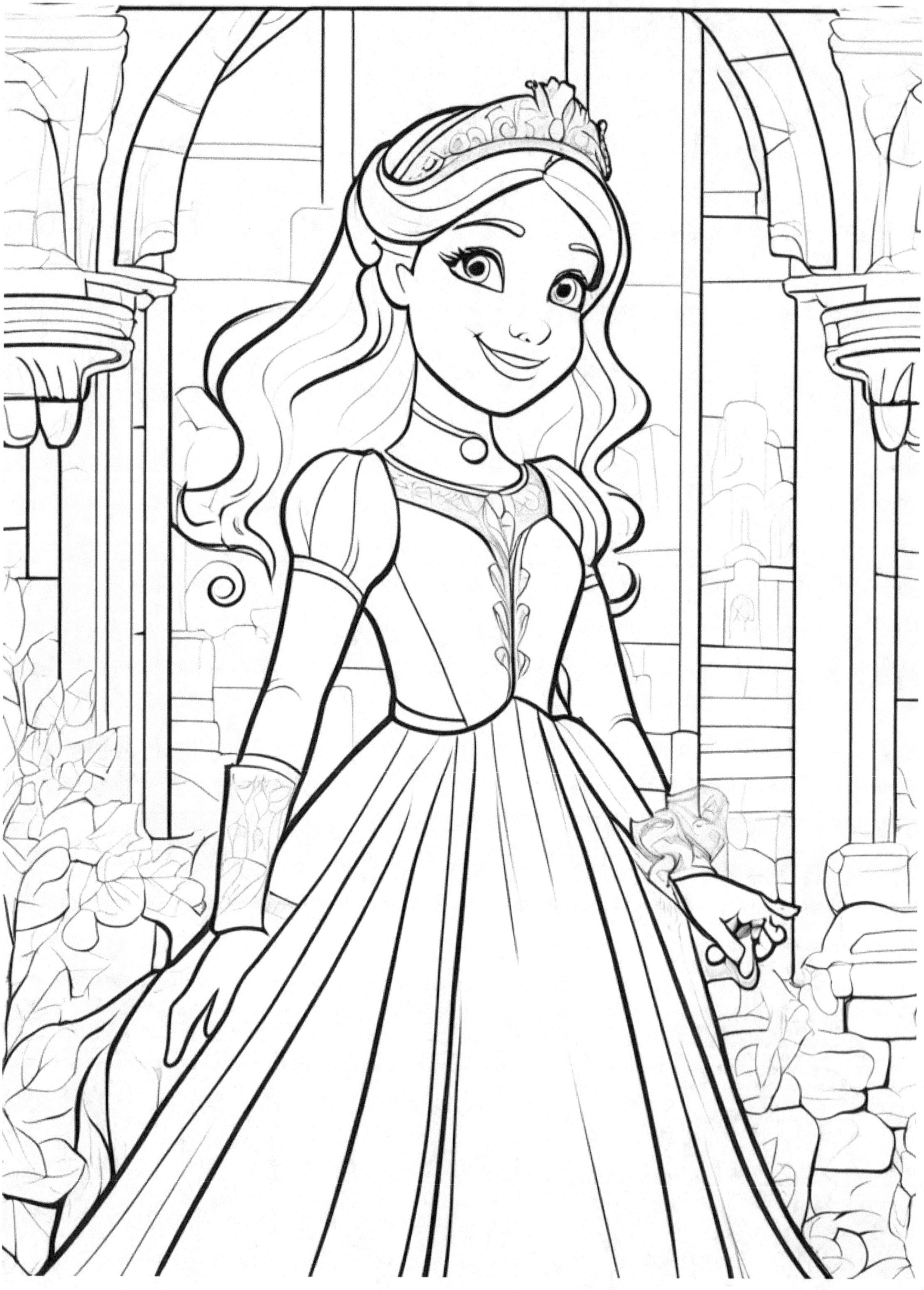

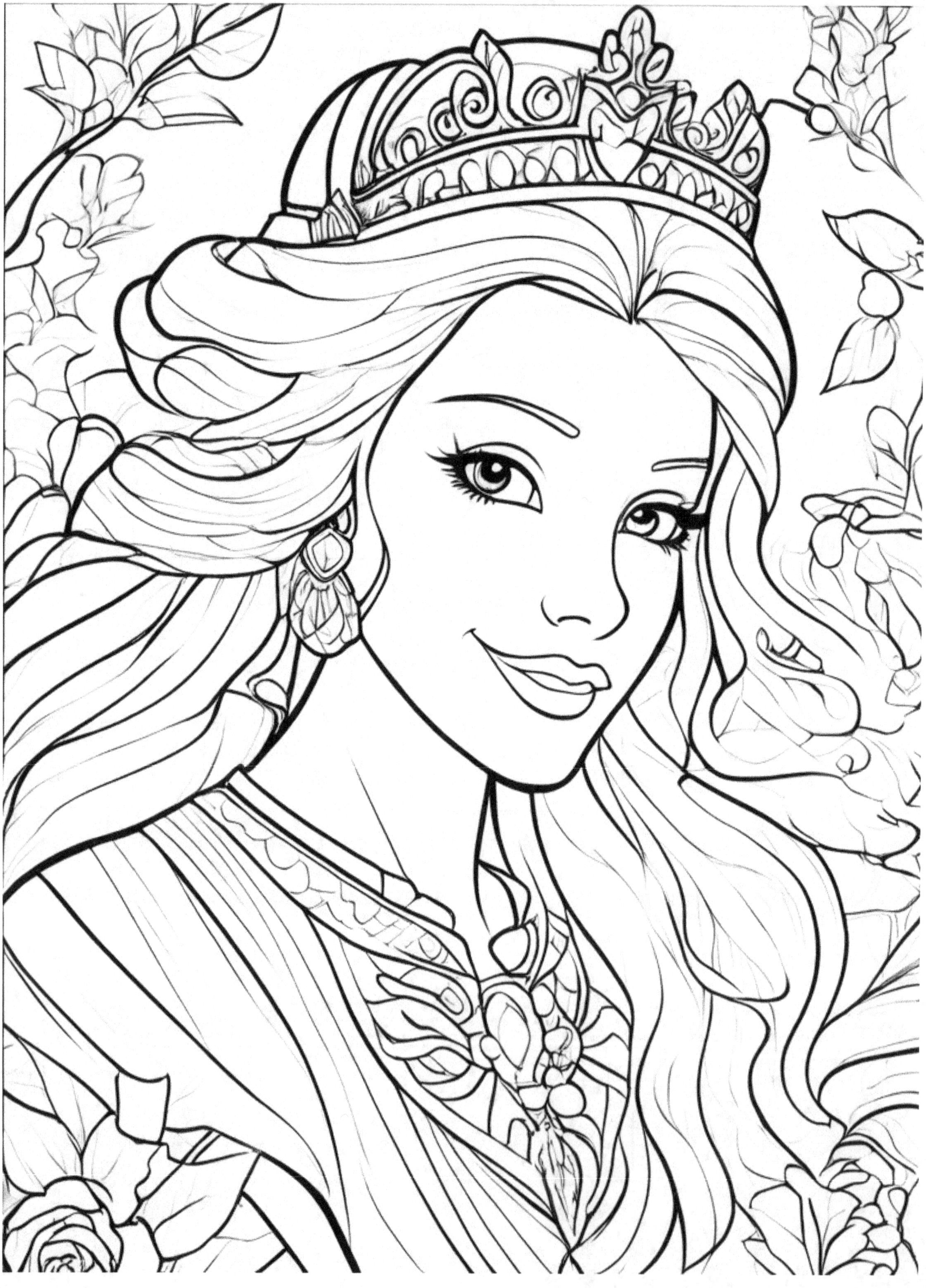

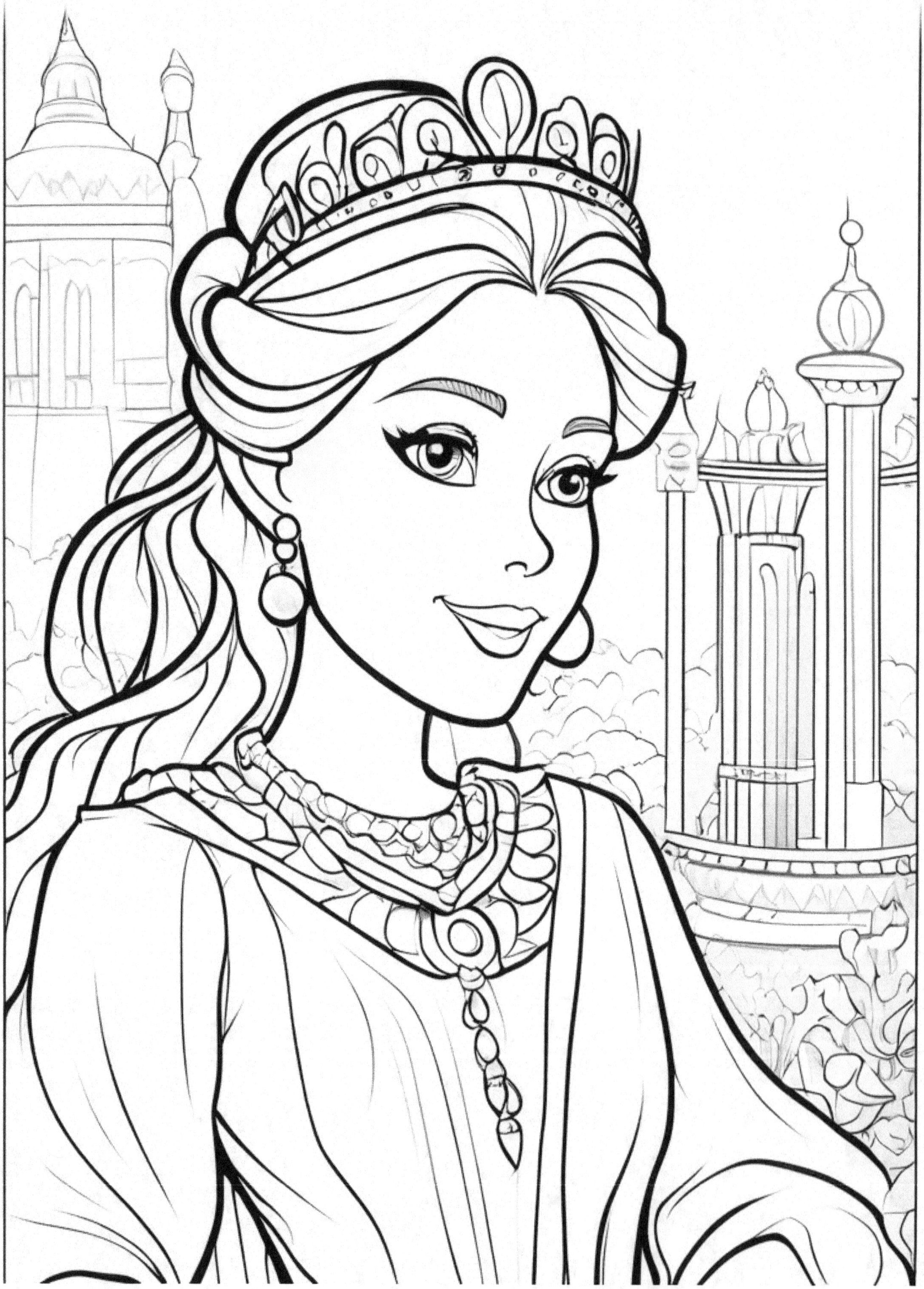

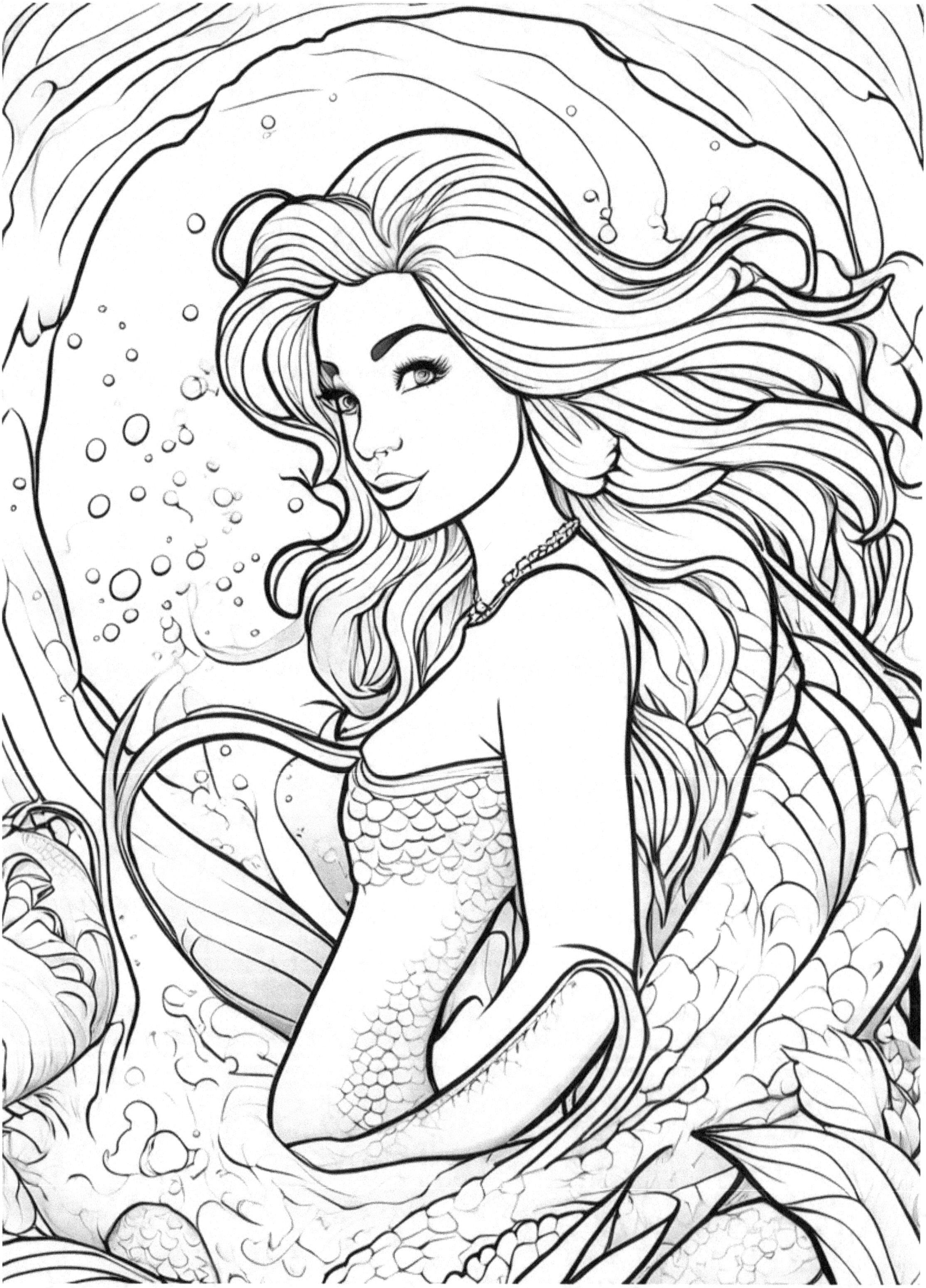

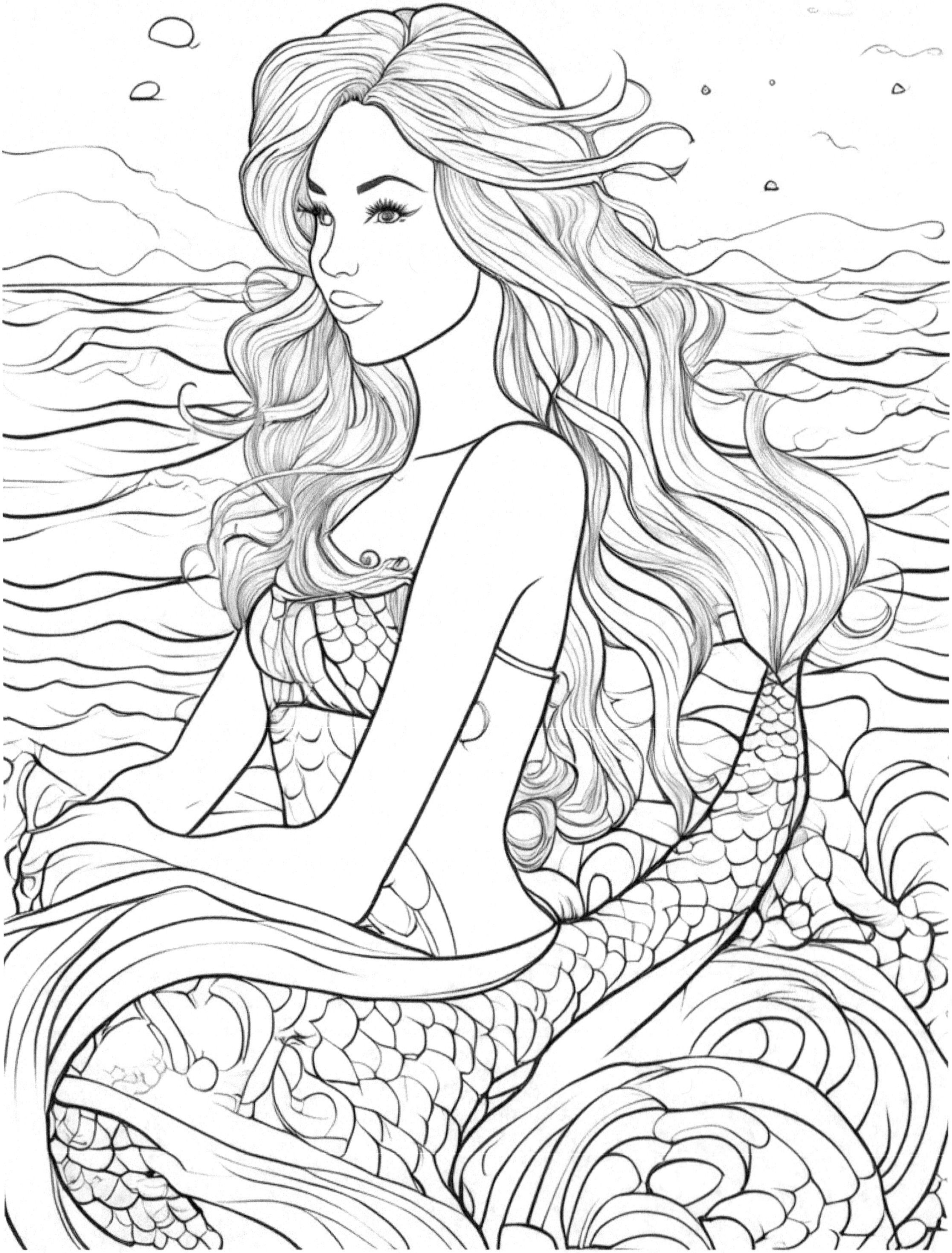

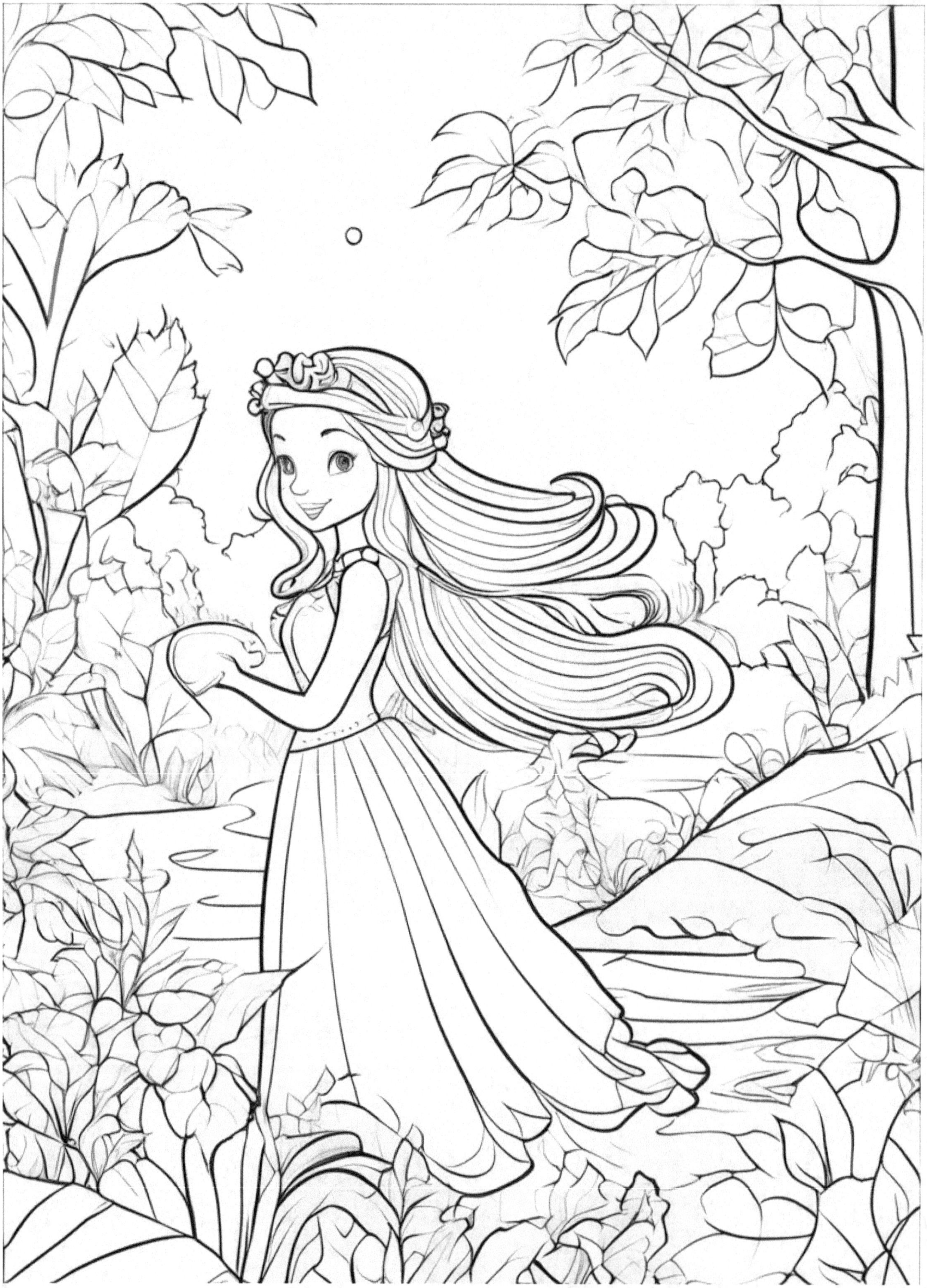

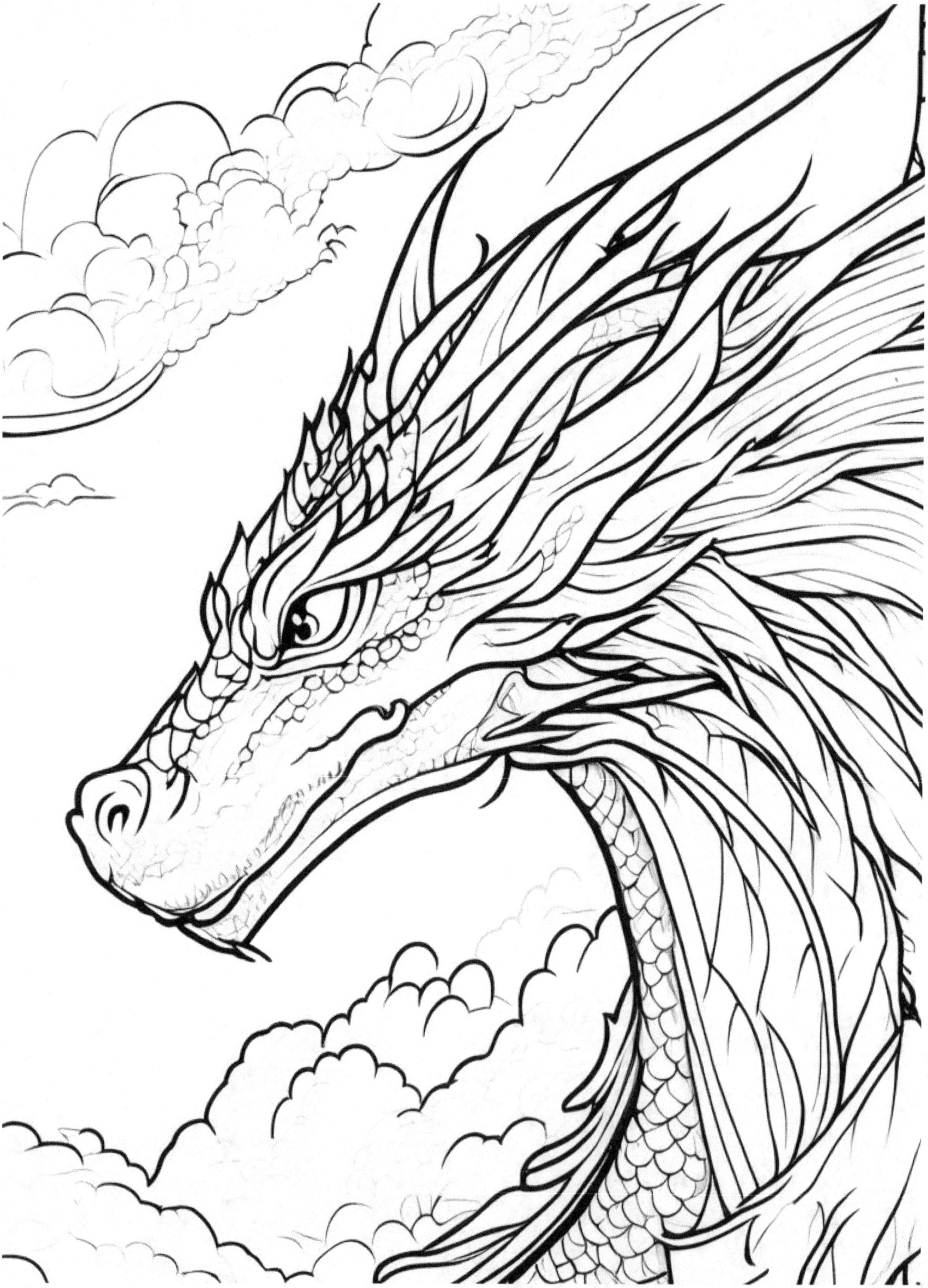

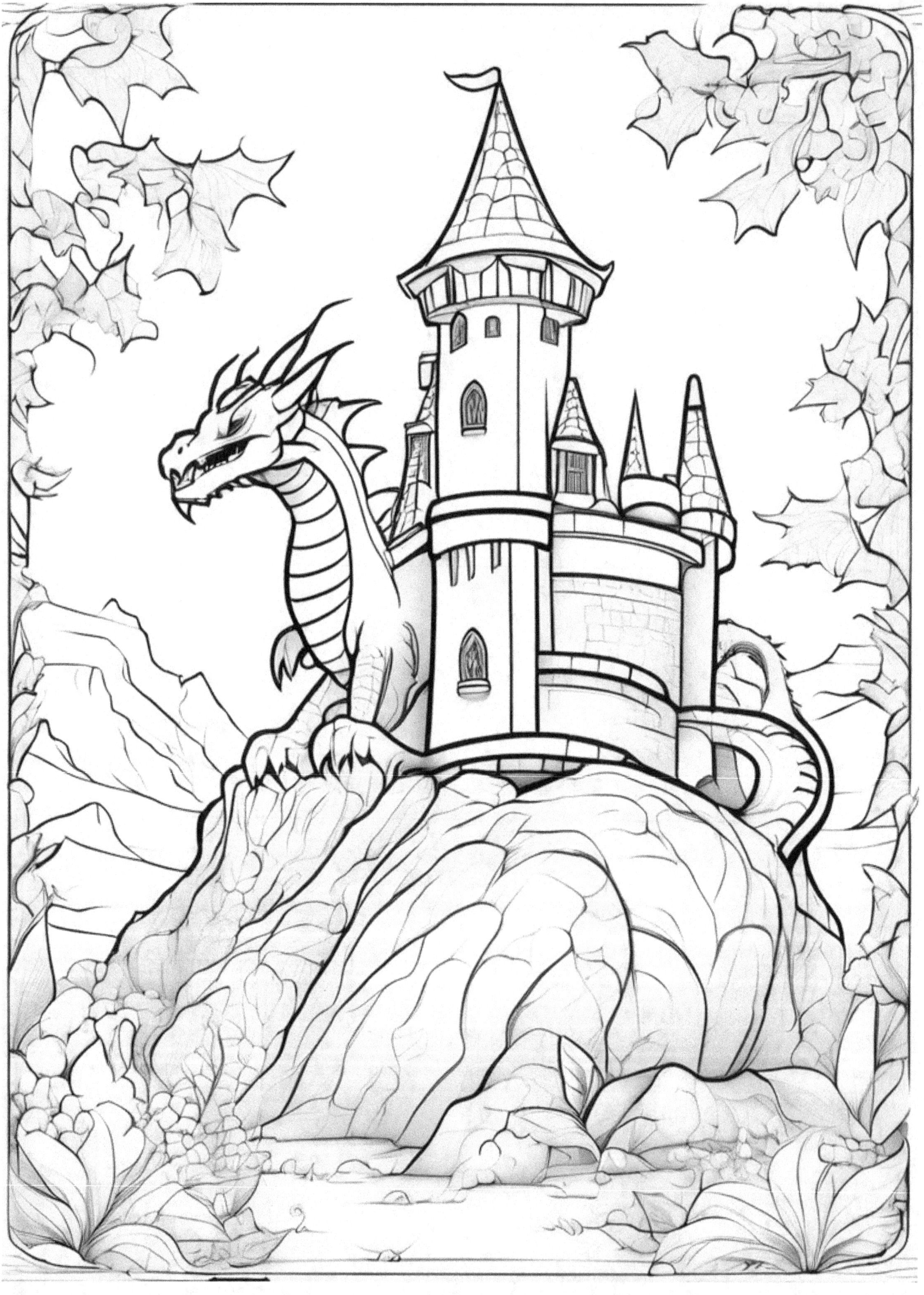

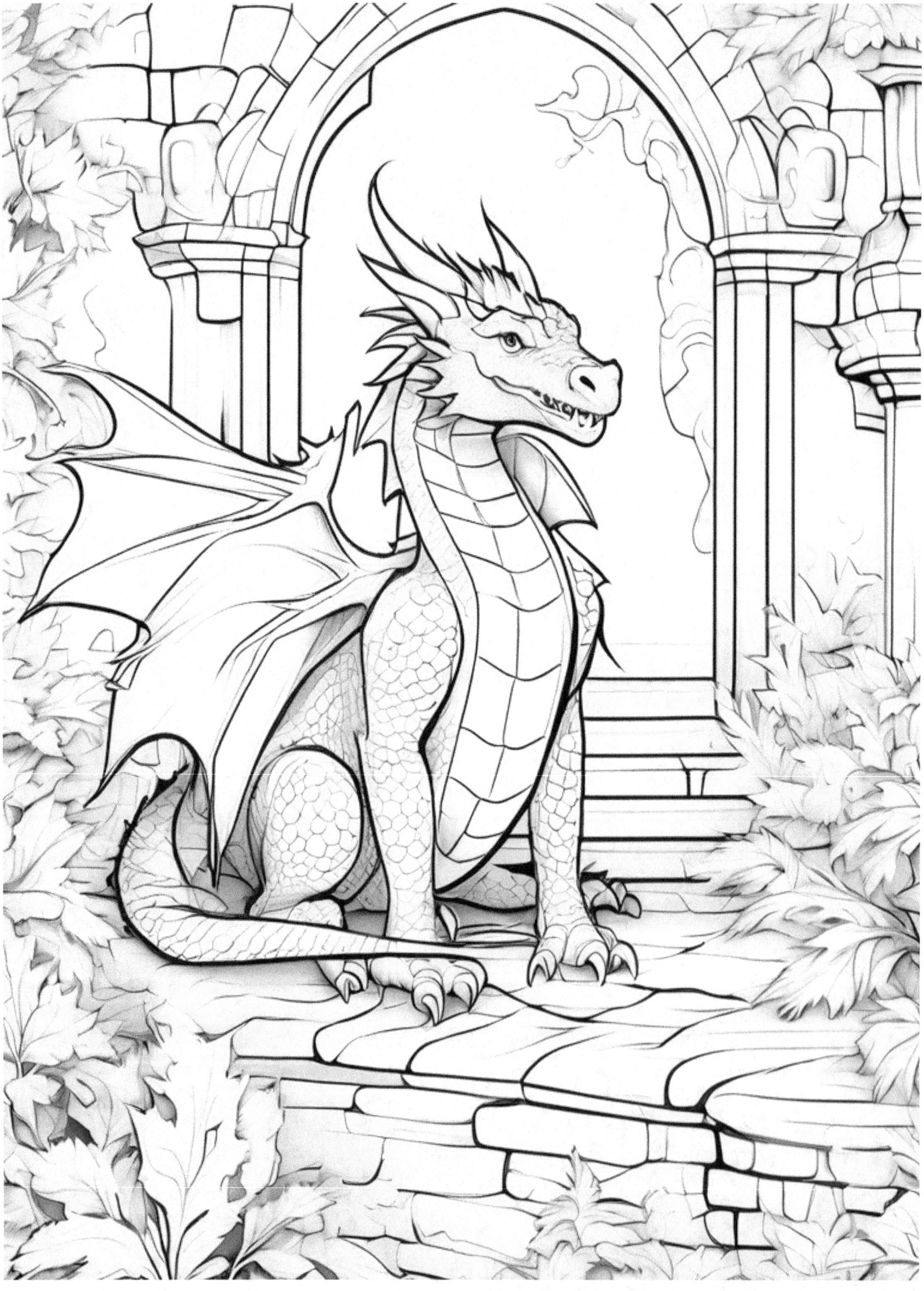

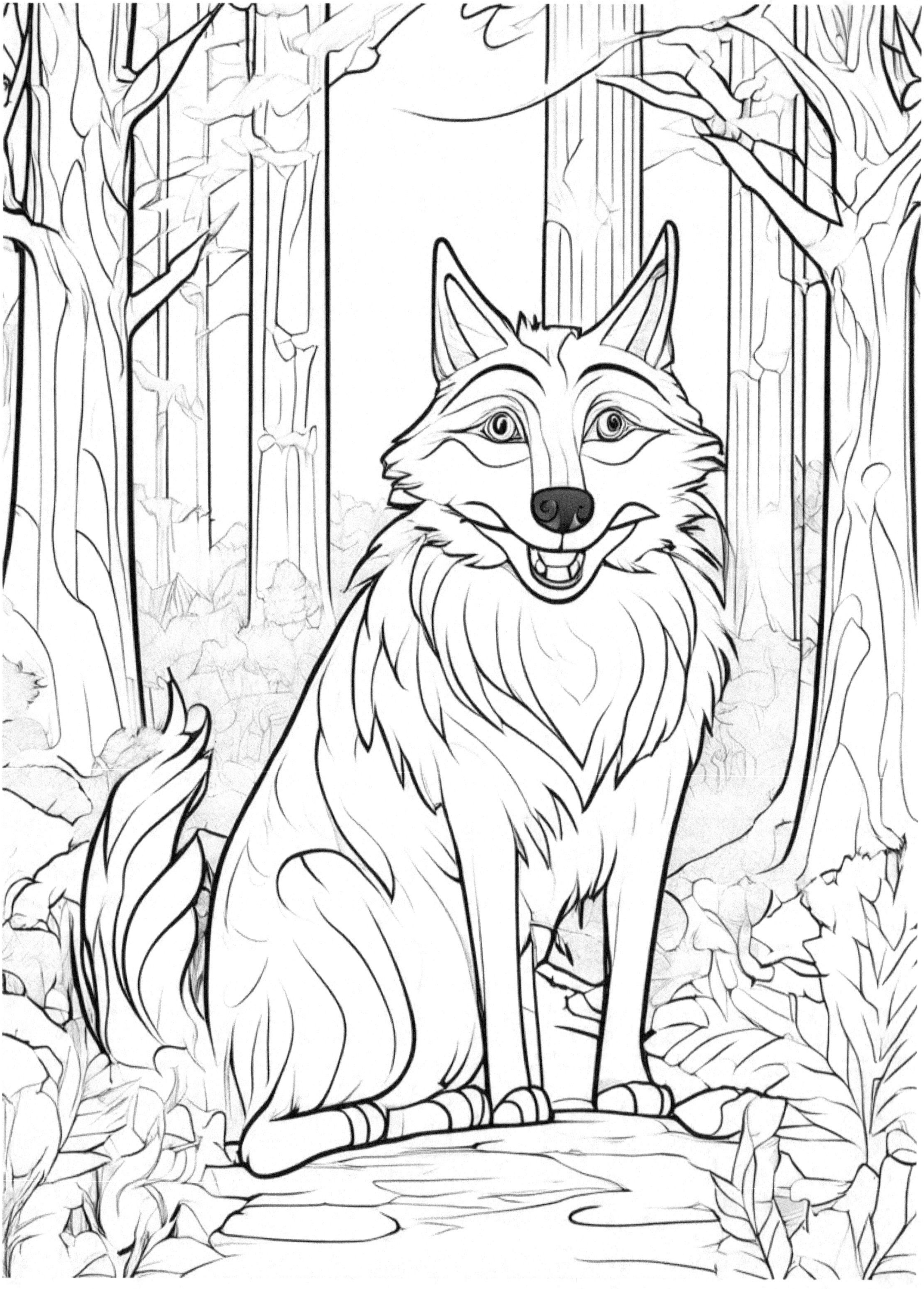

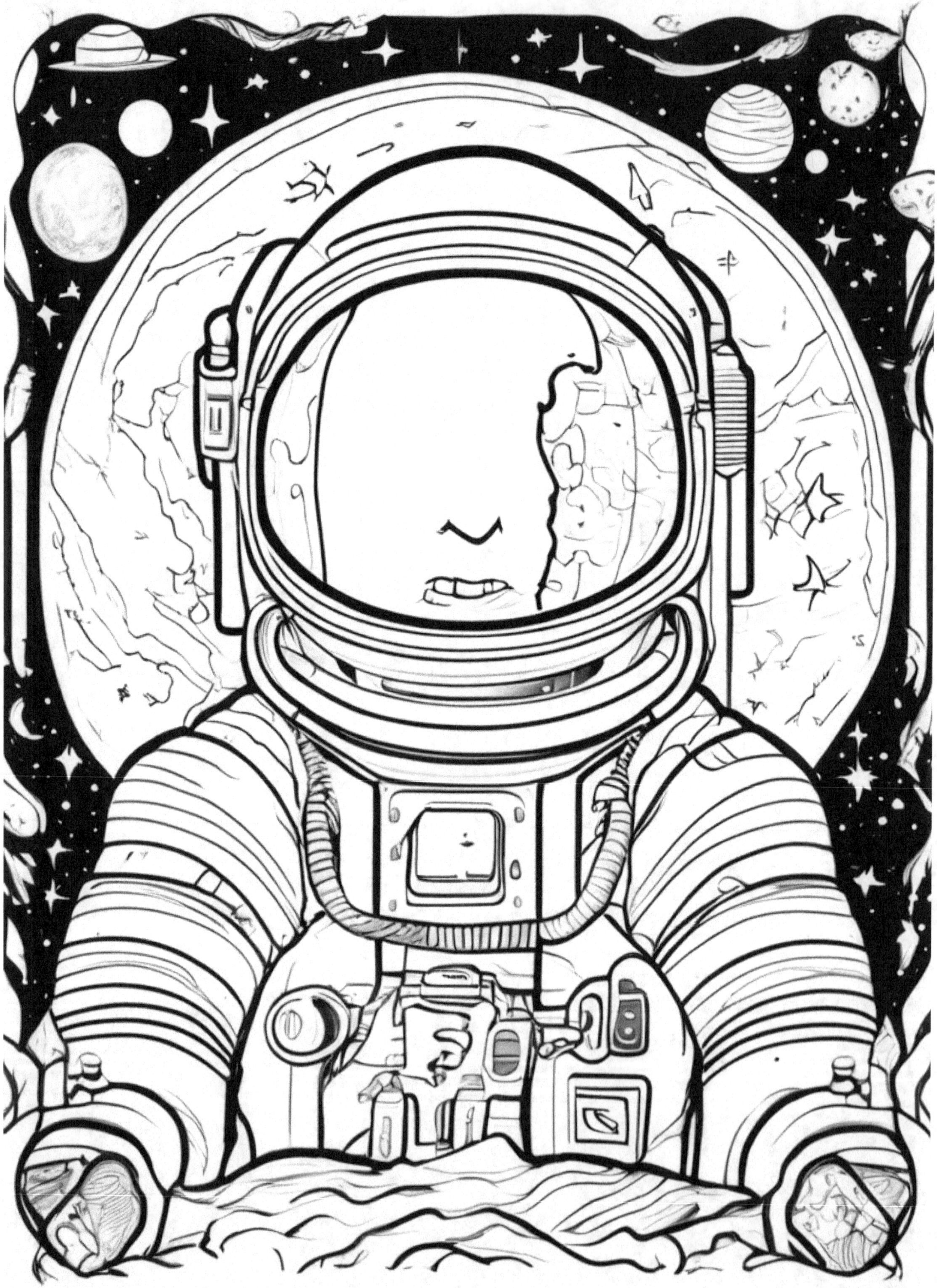

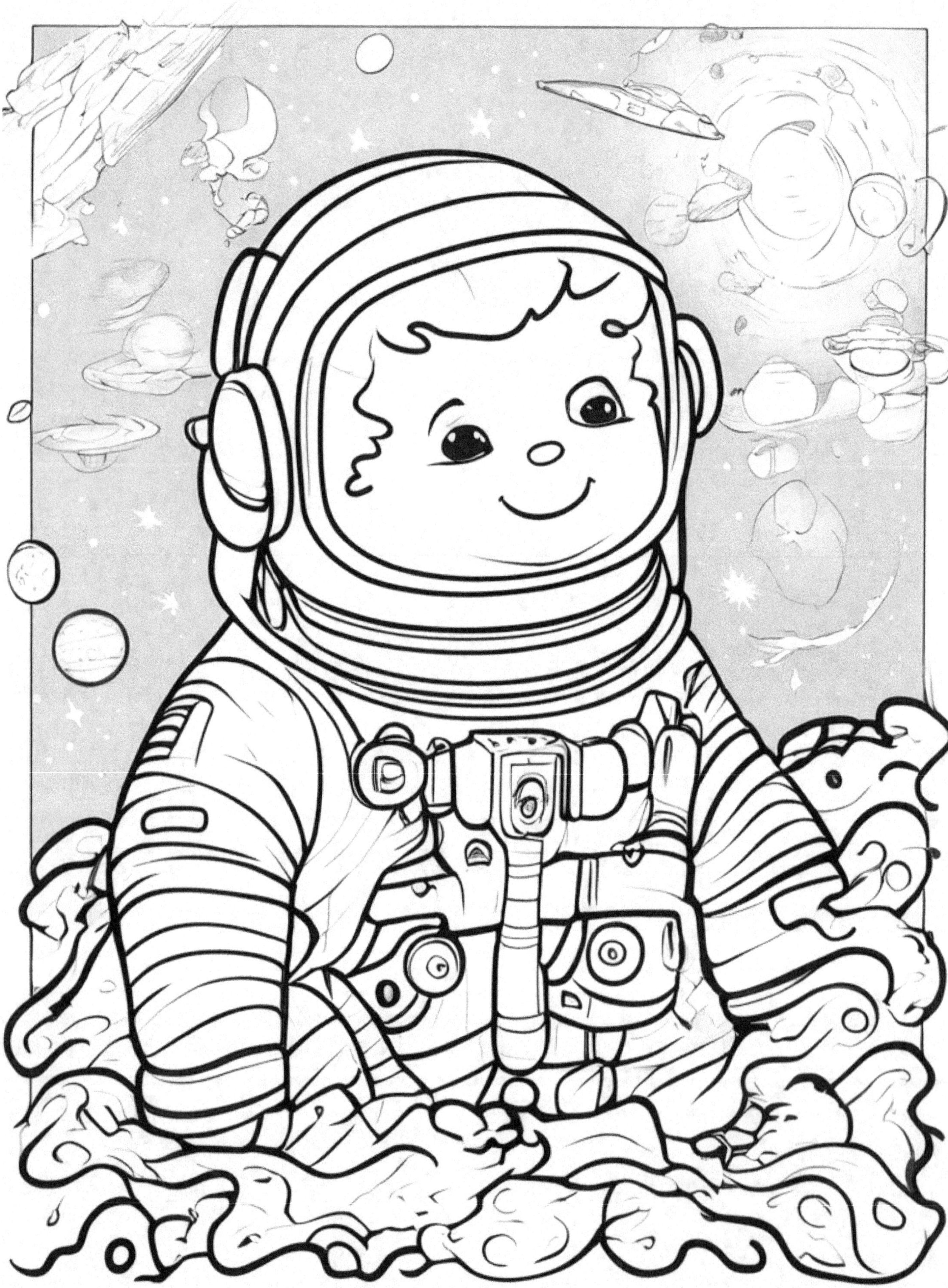

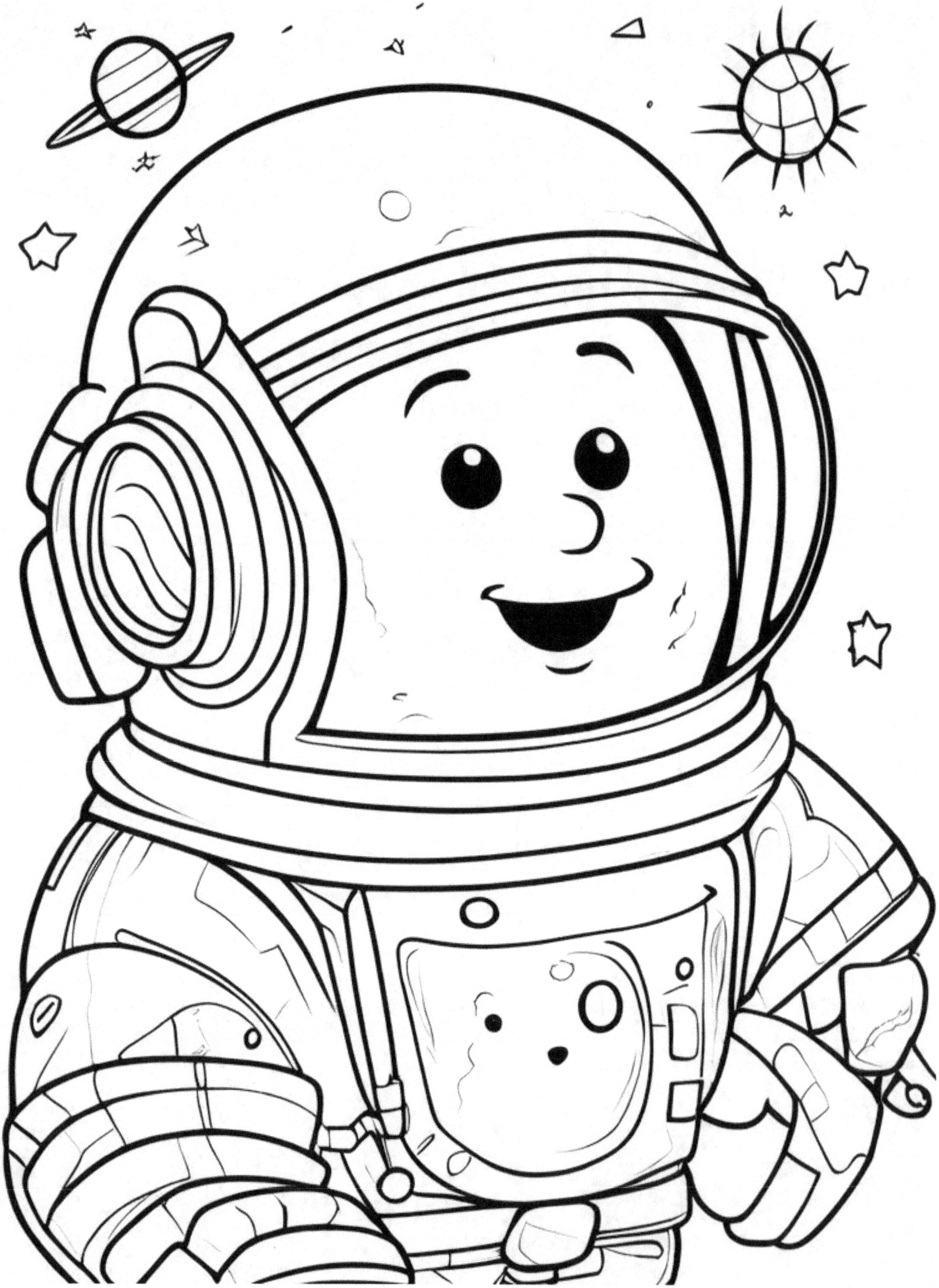

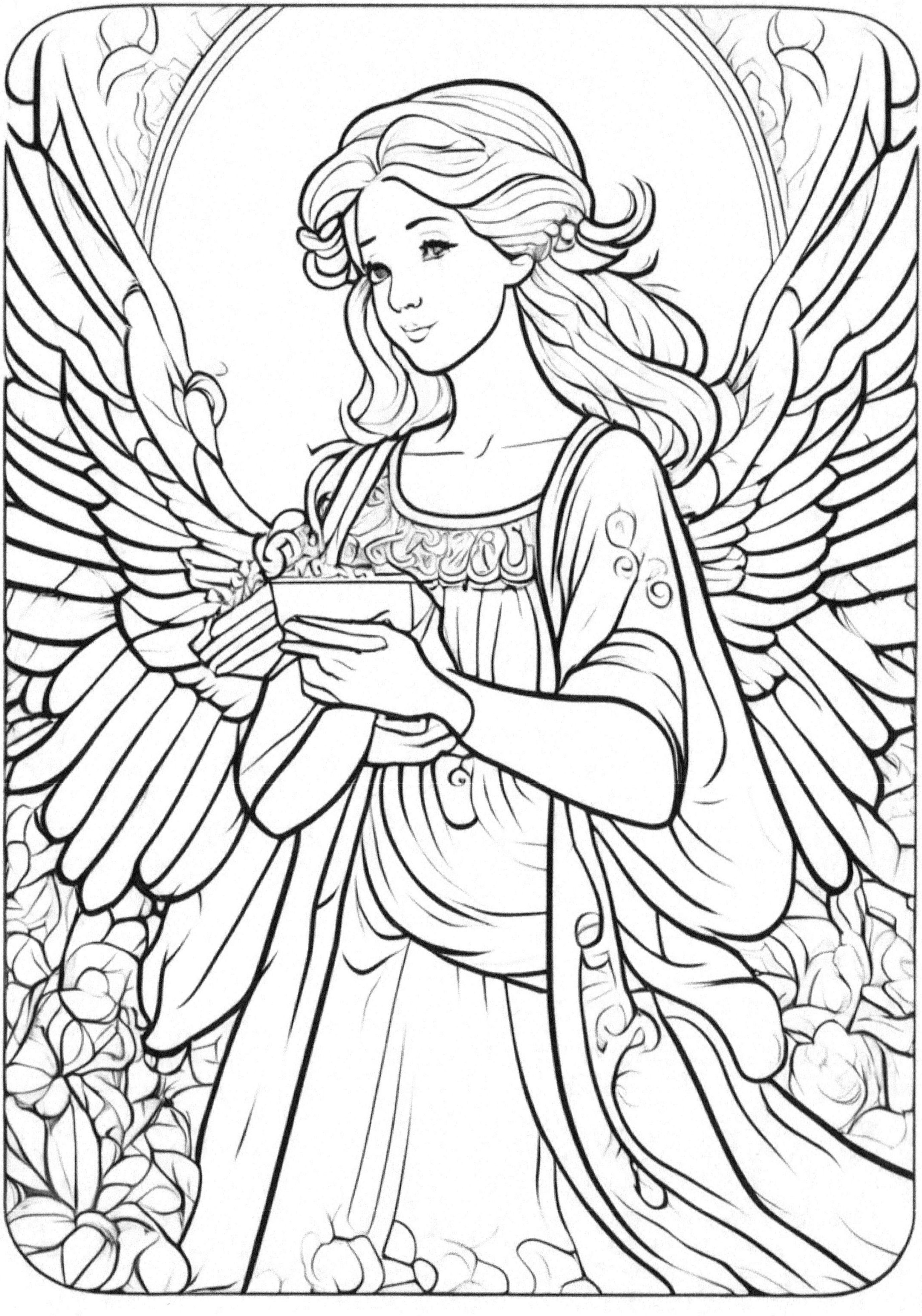

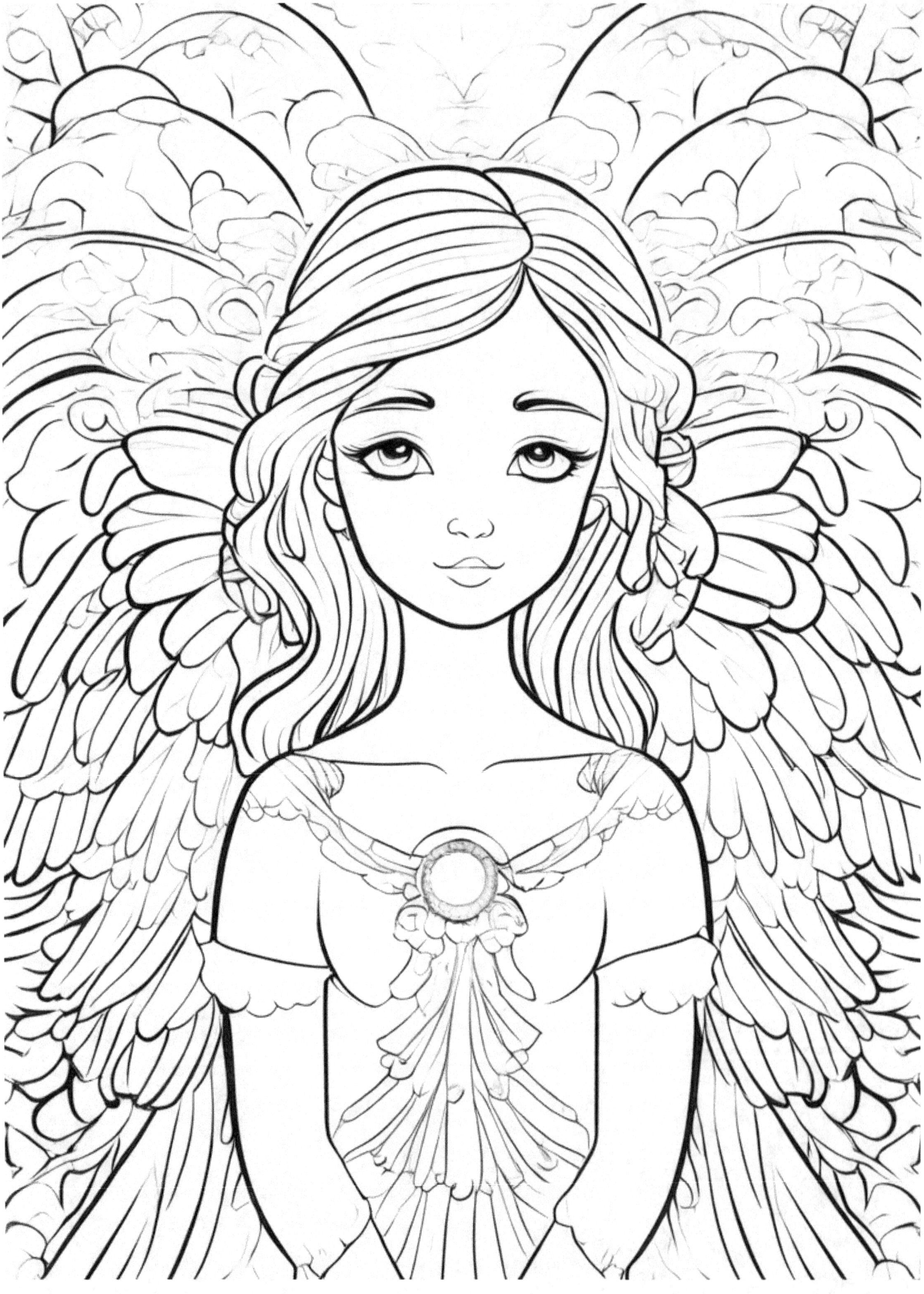

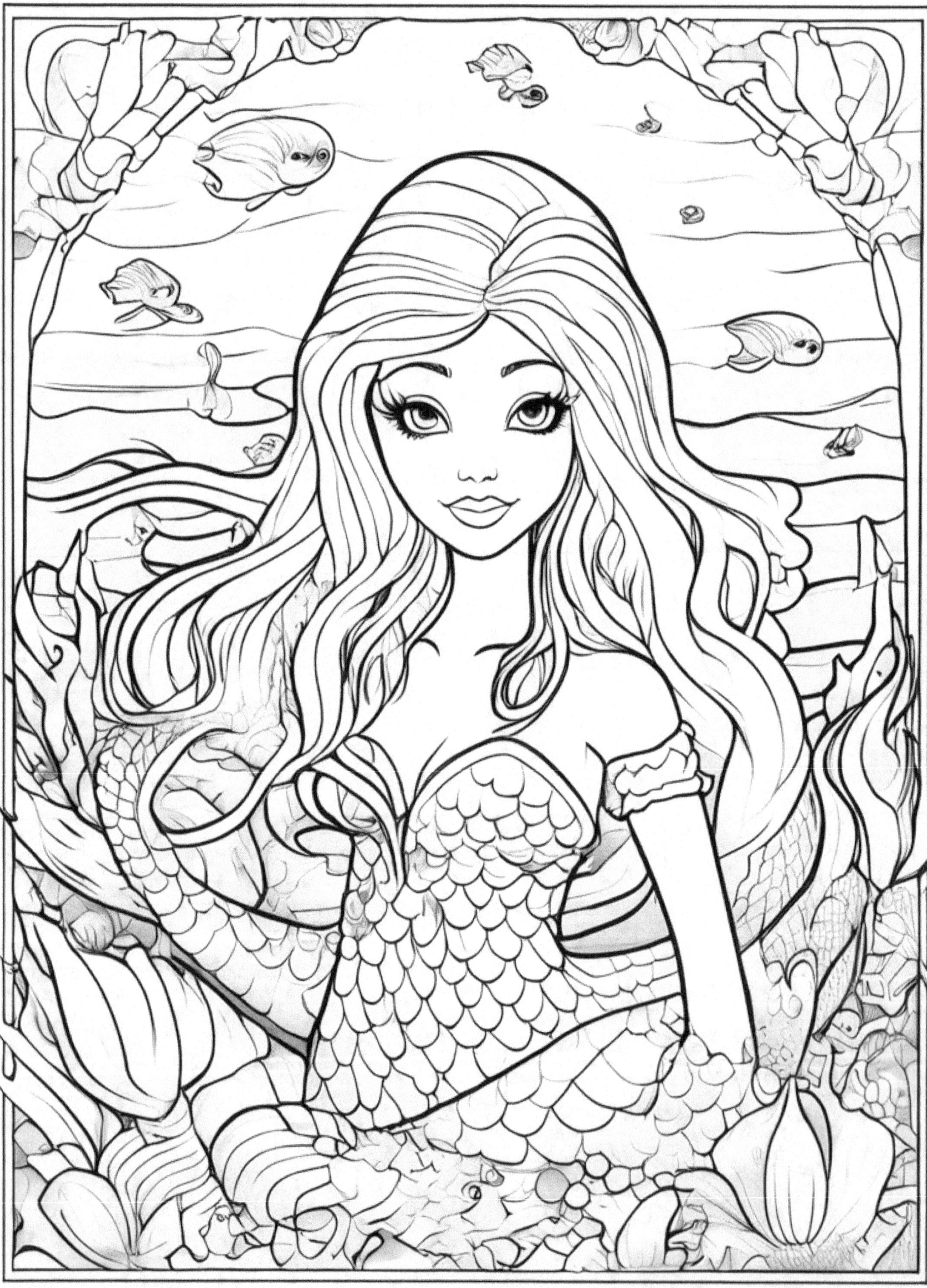

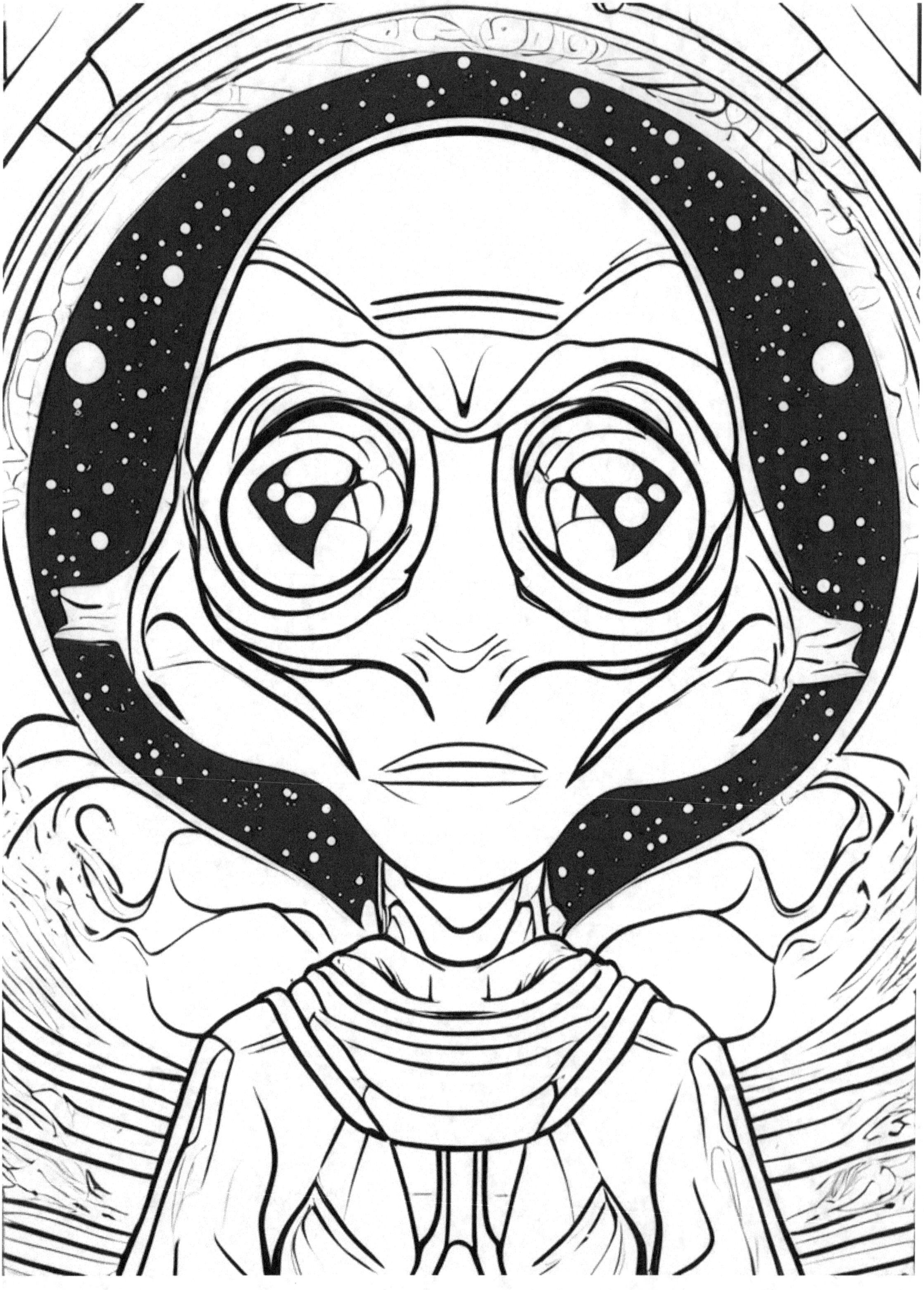

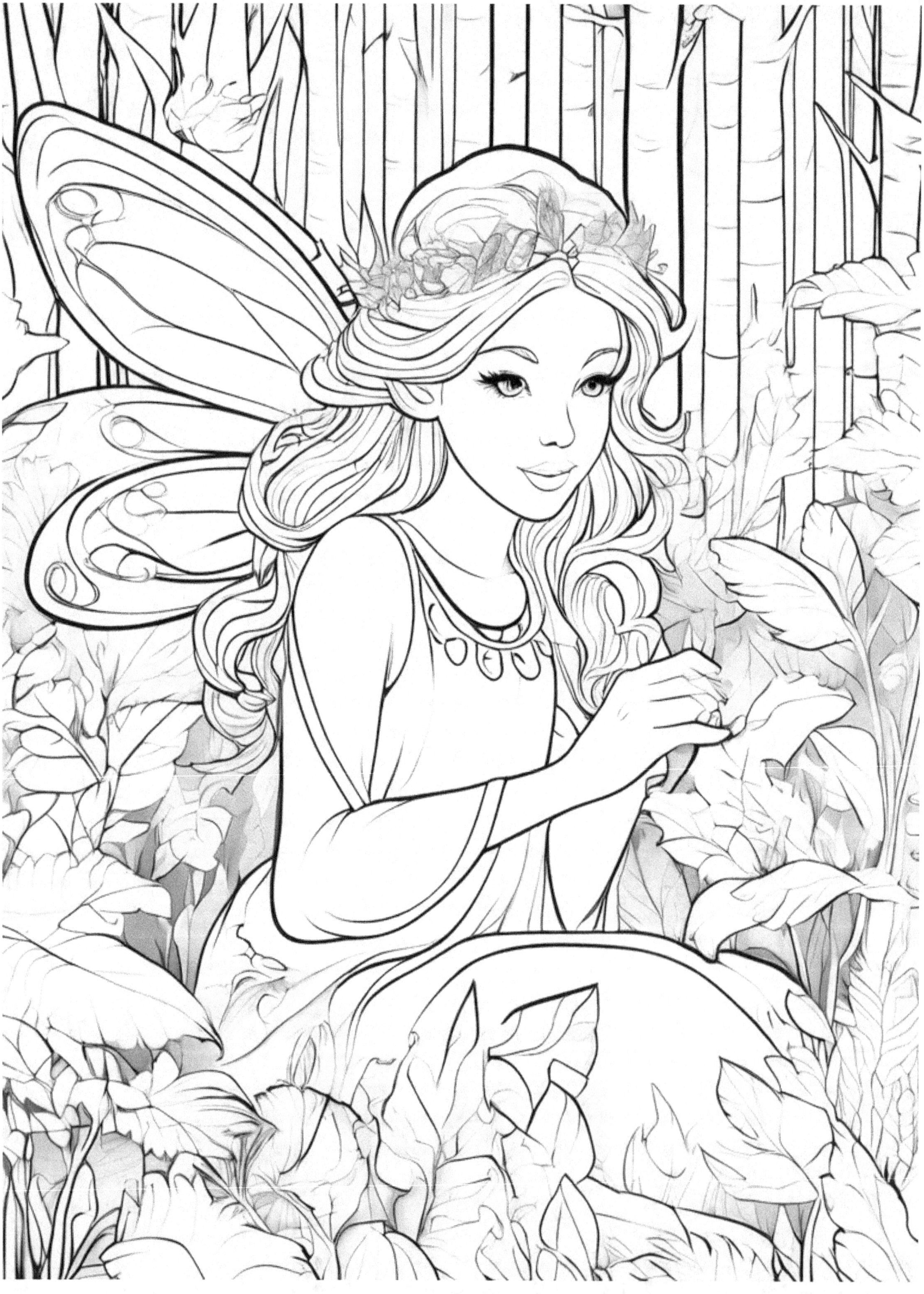

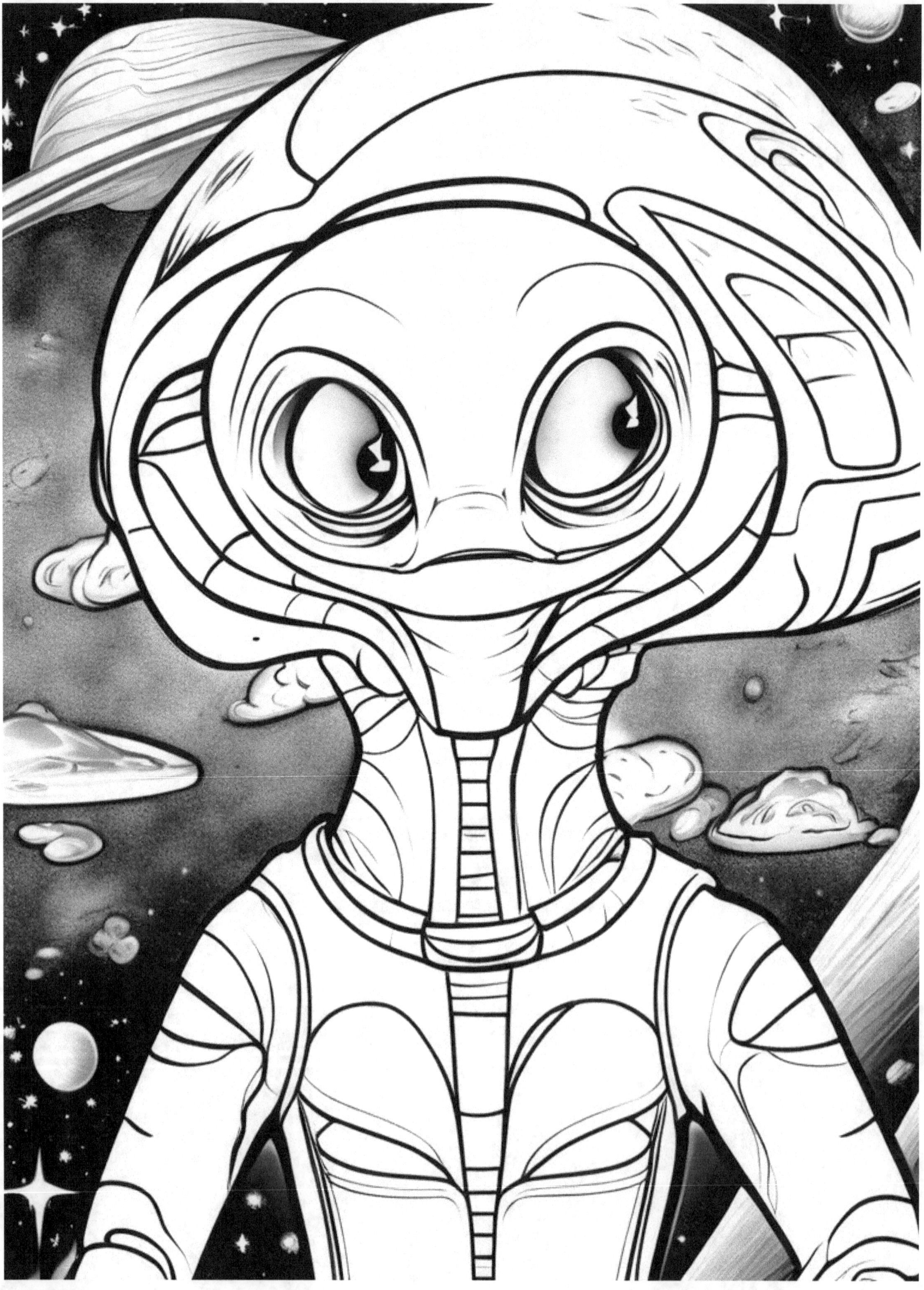

www.ingramcontent.com/pod-product-compliance
Lightning Source LLC
Chambersburg PA
CBHW082217220526
45470CB00010B/3199
* 9 7 9 8 3 2 5 2 0 1 9 6 7 *